The University of Michigan
Center for Chinese Studies

Michigan Monographs in Chinese Studies
No. 54

The Red Spears, 1916-1949

by Tai Hsüan-chih
translated by Ronald Suleski
introduction by Elizabeth Perry

Ann Arbor
Center for Chinese Studies
The University of Michigan
1985

Open access edition funded by the National Endowment for the Humanities/
Andrew W. Mellon Foundation Humanities Open Book Program.

Printed and bound by CPI Group (UK) Ltd, Croydon, CR0 4YY

ISBN 978-0-89264-060-7 (hardcover)
ISBN 978-0-89264-059-1 (paper)
ISBN 978-0-472-12791-7 (ebook)
ISBN 978-0-472-90187-6 (open access)

Contents

The Red Spears Reconsidered: An Introduction
Elizabeth J. Perry

Before Tai Hsüan-chih wrote his book on the Red Spear Society more than a decade ago, the subject of his study was a little understood movement that seemed of only passing interest to scholars of China — intriguing for its peculiar beliefs and rituals, perhaps, but hardly of central importance to modern Chinese history. Today, however, thanks in no small measure to the pioneering work of Professor Tai, the Red Spears have gained a secure niche in scholarship on modern China. Their numbers (reaching perhaps some three million participants at the height of the movement) and endurance (lasting intermittently for several decades) should stand as reason enough for the recent scholarly attention. But the Red Spears have generated interest for other reasons as well. As research into the history both of China's traditional rural rebellions and of her Communist revolution has developed over the past few years, the Red Spears have assumed increasing significance. A movement which bore marked similarities to earlier Chinese uprisings (most notably the Boxers), the Red Spears nevertheless operated in a later period of history (right through the middle of the twentieth century) which brought them in direct contact with Communist revolutionaries. An analysis of the Red Spears thus becomes important both for what it can tell us about longstanding patterns of rural rebellion in China, and for what it suggests about the nature of the Chinese revolution.

As the importance of the Red Spears has gained recognition, scholarly controversy over how to interpret the movement has also grown. The areas of dispute concern three basic aspects of the Red Spear Society: (1) origins, (2) social composition, and (3) relationship to revolution. On the first issue, there is disagreement over when and where the movement got underway. Although such matters may seem of only arcane interest, in fact they are closely connected to larger questions about the Red Spears' place in the tradition of

vii

Chinese popular protest: How was the Red Spear Society related to earlier secret society or sectarian groups, such as the White Lotus Society? Were the Red Spears descendants of the Boxers? The second issue concerns the nature of Red Spear members and leaders: Were these freeholding peasants, tenants, rich peasants, and/or landlords? In whose interests did the movement fight? Was it principally a class or community-based operation? Was it "conservative" or "progressive?" The third issue centers on the relationship between the Red Spear Society and the Chinese Communist revolution: Did the Red Spears facilitate or obstruct the course of the revolution?

Tai Hsüan-chih offers stimulating hypotheses on each of these three basic areas of dispute, thereby setting the framework for much of the scholarly debate which has ensued over the past decade and a half. On the question of origins, Professor Tai—who is also the author of a major study of the Boxer uprising—situates the Red Spears squarely in the Boxer tradition.[1] Tai sees the later movement as a "transformation" [yen-pien] of the Boxers, a process which he depicts by the metaphor of dead embers bursting into flame [ssu-hui fu-jan]. The assumption of continuity between Boxers and Red Spears is certainly a plausible one, particularly in light of the geographical proximity and similarities in ritualistic activities of the two movements. Moreover, the fact that many Red Spear leaders are known to have hailed originally from western Shantung—the region where the Boxers first got underway—lends further credibility to the continuity hypothesis. Still, the assumption of precise links between the two uprisings remains to be demonstrated. Professor Tai suggests that the Red Spears originated in the same counties of Shantung where the Boxers had first been active, only fifteen years after the earlier movement had been suppressed. However, inasmuch as a number of sources suggest different dates and places of birth for the movement, we are advised to exercise some caution in drawing the Boxer-Red Spear link.[2] But Tai Hsüan-chih argues for more than geographical or temporal connections; he also contends that the two movements shared a common organizational ancestor: the local militia. Here Tai is extending the line of argument advanced in his earlier book on the Boxers—an argument which holds that the village militia, rather than the sectarian White Lotus Society, was the institutional foundation of the movement.

In his earlier study, Professor Tai attempts to establish that the Boxers were an outgrowth of local defense forces [hsiang-t'uan] whose aim was to provide protection against rampant banditry. As part of the "orthodox" militia establishment, the Boxers were antagonistic to sectarian groups such as the White Lotus. Tai is certainly correct in asserting that the Boxers were not identical to White Lotus sectarians (or to allegedly White Lotus-affiliated groups such as the I-ho-ch'üan of the late eighteenth century); we know, for example, that Boxers did not worship the central deities of the White Lotus faith—just as White Lotus adherents paid no special homage to the heroes of Chinese fiction toward whom a good deal of Boxer ritualistic behavior was directed. Nevertheless, recent research by Susan Naquin shows that Professor Tai is mistaken in characterizing the White Lotus as a unified organization whose local branches "responded in unison to central commands." Furthermore, he errs in arguing that the invulnerability cult (which was a cornerstone of both Boxer and Red Spear ritual) was entirely foreign to the White Lotus tradition. Instead, it seems clear that methods of fighting intended to induce invulnerability (such as the "Armor of the Golden Bell") were well known among White Lotus believers.[3] During the White Lotus-inspired Wang Lun uprising of 1774 which occurred in western Shantung (home of both Boxers and Red Spears in later centuries), the rebels used magical charms to try to ensure invulnerability against government armaments. They chanted "guns will not fire," while women believers waved white fans in an apparent attempt to ward off enemy bullets.[4] Since similar practices reappeared in the Boxer and Red Spear movements, the earlier precedents are of considerable interest. Professor Tai is no doubt correct in pointing out that an important foundation of early Boxer strength lay in the institution of the local militia, but as Philip Kuhn has noted, the fact that a group called itself a local militia is not proof of its orthodox, anti-sectarian character.[5]

All of this is not to argue that either the Boxers or Red Spears were simply offshoots of the White Lotus; in fact mounting evidence suggests that both groups were often quite hostile to White Lotus members. Yet despite expressions of animosity against individual sectarians, it is clear that Boxers and Red Spears did draw inspiration from elements of the "heterodox" tradition. Indeed this question of the precise relationship of the Red Spears to the "Little Tradition" of rural China is a subject which has elicited increasing attention from scholars in recent years (as I will discuss below). If the origins of the Red Spears are still obscure, the social composition of the movement is somewhat better understood. Professor Tai has made a major contribution by correctly identifying the bulk of Red Spear leaders as drawn from the ranks of rich peasants, landlords and gentry. This important fact helps, I believe, to explain some of the ways in which the Red Spears departed from earlier sectarian groups in North China. As Tai notes, for example, women were excluded from Red Spear activities. Women were not permitted to attend ritual ceremonies and were even forbidden to make the protective stomach bands worn by Red Spears in battle; female meddling, the Red Spears believed, would vitiate their magical invulnerability. This absence of women is in striking contrast to the major role which women had played in many White Lotus sects. The exclusion may well reflect the Confucian mentality of Red Spear leaders, drawn as they were from the rural elite. References in Red Spear regulations to such Confucian values as filial piety lend further support to this hypothesis.[6]

As Professor Tai makes clear, early Red Spear operations were directed primarily against bandits. Over time, however, both the targets and the composition of the movement grew more complex. Marauding warlord troops and rapacious tax collectors prompted the Red Spears to fight against soldiers and government officials as well as bandits. Tai offers interesting information on the tax burden during the Republican period, although the data must be treated with caution in light of the imprecise statistics available for the period. (One wonders, for example, just how Professor Tai arrived at his conclusion that the people of Shantung in 1927 paid more than four times the taxes paid in the United States that year.) Despite ambiguities in the figures, it seems clear that onerous surtaxes were being imposed in much of the North China countryside. And, as Tai points out, Red Spear resistance was directed at these surcharges rather than at the land tax itself. Seeing the latter as a legitimate "emperor's tax" (albeit years after the imperial system had been overturned), the Red Spears objected only to the newly imposed surcharges. Theirs was thus a conservative position which harked back to earlier days for its moral standards.

In time, the purely defensive character of the Red Spear movement was somewhat modified. Professor Tai observes that leadership came increasingly to be usurped by local bullies, who sometimes converted their groups into bandit outfits. As the translator of this volume states in his introduction, Tai Hsüan-chih is uncertain about just how to evaluate the role of the Red Spears. This ambiguity, a natural consequence of the very complicated nature of Red Spear composition and activities, has also troubled historians in the People's Republic of China. Should the Red Spears be judged a "progressive" or "reactionary" force in Chinese history? If Professor

Tai holds the local bully element responsible for a deterioration in
Red Spear discipline, PRC historians have been even more concerned
with landlord-rich peasant involvement in the movement. As we will
see below, recognition of this difficulty has led to a negative
assessment of the Red Spears in recent Chinese scholarship.

This brings us to the third area of controversy surrounding the
Red Spear movement: its relationship to revolution. Professor Tai's
interesting discussion of connections between various Red Spear
groups and both Communist and Kuomintang forces in North China
demonstrates the complexity of the issue. Yet, as Tai suggests, a
pattern can be deciphered amidst the welter of confusing historical
detail; generally speaking, the Red Spears were friend to neither the
Nationalists nor the Communists. To be sure, the Red Spear
movement — concerned as it was to protect rural villages from outside
threats — played a useful role in resisting Japanese invaders. But
such a position scarcely rendered the Red Spears more hospitable to
other outsiders such as the Kuomintang or Communists. Although
occasional alliances were forged, on the whole the Red Spears posed
much more of an obstacle than an opportunity for revolutionary
cadres. Sabotage, betrayal, ambushes and outright military
confrontations were common rewards for the efforts of would-be
revolutionary organizers. Speculation as to the reasons for this
hostility (Red Spear ideology, organization, leadership, class
composition; Communist and Kuomintang approaches; etc.) has been
a source of lively scholarly debate in recent years.

Since the publication of Professor Tai's book, a number of other
studies of the Red Spears have appeared in China, Japan and the
United States. These works have added substantially both to our
factual knowledge of Red Spear operations and to an explanation of
the ancestry, development, and historical role of this enormous rural
uprising in early twentieth century China. Let us turn now to this
more recent scholarship, considering in turn its implications for Red
Spear origins, composition, and relationship to revolution.

Origins: Institutional and Religious

That the Red Spears began in North China as a self-defense
movement against bandit and warlord rampages of the early
Republican period is beyond dispute. The connection between this
movement and other earlier and contemporary defense groups is,
however, more controversial. Tai Hsüan-chih depicts the Red Spears

as a child of the Boxers and grandchild of the rural militia. Tracing the history of the militia back to the Northern Sung, Tai suggests that this institution became especially active after the mid-nineteenth century in response to the Taiping Rebellion. Although the establishment of militia was initially encouraged by the government authorities, some of these groups later became vehicles for anti-state activities. Known as "militia bandits" [*t'uan-fei* or *lien-chuan hui-fei*], such groups launched tax revolts and in some cases even attempted to assume control of county governments. In Tai's view, both the Boxers and the Red Spears were direct descendants of this nineteenth-century development.

Japanese scholar Mitani Takashi adopts a similar analysis in an important article on the Honan Red Spears published in 1974, only a year after publication of Tai's book. Mitani contends that the Red Spears grew out of village self-defense forces such as the *lien-chuang-hui*. When these groups met with official repression, suggests Mitani, they went underground and assumed a more religious flavor. In his view, the addition of religious beliefs helped the Red Spears to attract marginal elements and mitigated the class contradictions that might otherwise have inhibited cross-class cooperation.[7]

A very different interpretation of the Red Spears' relationship to pre-existing self-defense units is outlined in a 1976 article by Baba Takeshi. Baba rejects Mitani's characterization of the Red Spears as an outgrowth of *lien-chuang-hui* with religious trappings, and argues that two different types of rural militia must be distinguished. The people's militia [*min-t'uan*] were, according to Baba, spontaneously organized by villagers. The *lien-chuang-hui* [united village associations], on the other hand, were established by provincial or county fiat from the top down. Baba contends that the Red Spears developed at the expense of the people's militia, which was undermined in the process. The *lien-chuang-hui*, however, remained as officially approved institutions. Whereas Red Spears often engaged in tax protests and attacks on provincial-level powerholders such as warlords and armies, the *lien-chuang-hui* limited their opposition to bandits and did not challenge the political authorities.[8]

A subsequent article by Mitani counters this contention and argues that no sharp line can be drawn between official and popular defense forces. Baba, charges Mitani, has confused official policy with reality. In actuality, *lien-chuang-hui* could also serve as the foundation of anti-state activity.[9]

Regardless of which side of the debate one prefers, the informed interchange between these young Japanese scholars highlights the complexity of the relationship between the Red Spears (or, for that matter, the Boxers) and pre-existing forms of rural defense. The militarization of late nineteenth- to early twentieth-century China was both a product of state encouragement and a response to state incompetence. Just how this process interacted with popular religious traditions to give rise to movements such as the Boxers and Red Spears is not yet fully understood.

As Professor Tai points out, neither the Boxers nor the Red Spears should be seen as branches of the White Lotus sect. For Tai, the religious origins of these movements lie rather in the polytheistic, "superstitious" atmosphere that permeated the Chinese countryside. This mindset, he believes, was inculcated over thousands of years with the encouragement of the imperial rulers. All dynastic founders, for example, claimed to have entered this world by means of a miraculous, supernatural birth which served as one authentication of their hold on the Mandate of Heaven. A widespread belief in spirit possession, charms, and invulnerability laid the groundwork, according to Tai, for Red Spear religious practices.

The origins and significance of these religious practices have been a matter of some dispute. The writings of Mitani, or for that matter my own writings, portray Red Spear religion in basically functionalist terms — as a useful medium for facilitating cross-class participation.[10] Baba, however, assigns a more energizing role to Red Spear religion. To be sure, Baba, like Tai Hsüan-chih, eschews a White Lotus-Red Spear identity. He admits that the Red Spears lacked the beliefs in a Maitreyan savior or an afterlife that were such central elements in the White Lotus faith. Nevertheless, Baba asserts that the messianic claims of some Red Spear leaders and the invulnerability cult of their followers were essentially religious. Faith in the supernatural allowed peasants to transcend the boundaries of their otherwise parochial world and enter a new, expanded mode of existence. In Baba's view, Red Spear rituals transformed the peasants' "village communitarian visions" [sonraku no kyōdō gensō] into "religious sect communitarian visions" [shūkyō kessha no kyōdō gensō].[11]

Baba is, however, frank in acknowledging that the paucity of primary source materials on Red Spear mentality makes it impossible to determine with confidence the precise content and meaning of Red Spear beliefs. Whether, for example, the Red Spears really accepted the idea of kalpas (a Buddhist concept of long-term historical transformation which was central to White Lotus eschatology) is uncertain.[12]

An attempt to get closer to an understanding of Red Spear mentality by making use of additional sources — most notably novels published in the People's Republic — has recently been undertaken by Ralph Thaxton. Thaxton boldly asserts that the Red Spears were "openly proclaiming their pursuit of a Buddhist-inspired antigovernment apocalypse."[13] For Thaxton, the Red Spears espoused a "rebellious folk eschatology" which reflected an "antistate, and by association anti-Confucian folklore. . . fermenting among the peasantry."[14] Unfortunately, Thaxton's innovative approach is marred by the careless use of suspect sources. Novels written by state-sponsored intellectuals well after the victory of the revolution would seem a questionable guide to peasant mentality during the revolutionary process.[15] And Thaxton's misreading of the sources is an even more serious problem.[16]

To criticize Thaxton's methodology is certainly not to deny the importance of his concerns. Scholars should indeed be more sensitive to the religious origins and meanings of Chinese peasant movements. Even historians in the P.R.C. admit a central role for religious inspiration among the Red Spears. An oral history project conducted by historians at Cheng-chou University in the Honan-Hupei area ascertained, for example, that the Red Spear Society in that region was "initially a religious organization which developed out of the Red Lotus Sect and worshipped Heavenly Master Chang." Informants recalled that the Red Spears' preparation for battle had involved complicated religious rituals. Before any military confrontation, the Red Spear boxing master — one shoulder bared — would grip a sword with his teeth while holding an eight-trigram flag in one hand and leading a goat with his other hand. Striding at the head of his ranks, he was followed by ordinary Red Spears holding swords or spears in one hand and towels or fans (to wave off enemy bullets) in the other. After reciting incantations, the master chopped off the goat's head and sprinkled its blood on the flag. When he had offered sacrifices to ensure divine protection, the master waved his flag and shouted while his followers sprinkled "five-precautions earth" — *wu-fang-t'u* — dirt which had been dug up from in front of Buddhist images in a temple, wrapped in a long piece of blue cloth, and worn around the believers' waists. Only when these procedures had been completed were the Red Spears ready for battle.[17]

That such rituals were important in building Red Spear commitment and solidarity seems clear. Whether they reflected "the peasants' radically democratic millenialist vision"[18] seems much more questionable. One can only hope that further oral histories (such as those conducted in former Boxer strongholds in the 1950s) will help to unravel the meaning of Red Spear beliefs. Relying on just such oral histories, Joseph Esherick has been able to distinguish two quite separate local Boxer traditions in Shantung, differentiated both by social composition and by religious ritual. In southwest Shantung, where the Boxers (known as the Big Sword Society) were led by landlords and rich peasants, charms were swallowed to induce invulnerability. By contrast, the peasant-led Spirit Boxers of northwest Shantung practiced a type of spirit possession whereby any member could speak with divine authority. Opening the door to universal deification, this ritual had important egalitarian implications.[19] Perhaps further field research on the Red Spears will reveal comparable patterns.

Social Composition and Organization

There is little doubt that the majority of Red Spear outfits were led by rural notables—landlords, rich peasants, or local strongmen. Equally indisputable is the fact that poor and middle peasants constituted the majority of rank and file Red Spear members. This cross-class composition, well delineated by Tai Hsüan-chih and confirmed by subsequent researchers, creates difficulties for analyzing the essential character of the movement. Should the Red Spears be seen as a class-based or community-based phenomenon? In either case, whose interests were served by the movement? Were the Red Spears "progressive" or "conservative"?

The leadership of the movement is certainly of critical importance in any assessment of its character. Mitani has argued, and I am inclined to agree, that the limitations of the Red Spears stemmed not from their religious beliefs, but from their domination by local powerholders.[20] Yet recent research has established that Red Spears leaders themselves were not a homogeneous group. A study of the Red Spear movement in the Hupei-Honan area makes clear that each Red Spear unit (known as a t'ang, this unit usually included some 100-150 members) had two types of leaders. One type, called "teachers" [hsüeh-tung], was in charge of the general management of the group. Such persons were usually lineage elders or other prestigeous individuals with close connections to landlords and gentry. The other type of leader, known as "boxing masters" [ch'üan-shih], was a very different sort. Often riff-raff from Shantung or Hopei, these people were invited into the community to teach martial arts and magic to local Red Spear members. Despite this division of leadership responsibilities, however, informants recall that "the Red Spear Society in the Hupei-Honan border area was a local military organization established by landlords for the purpose of protecting their reactionary control."[21] Able-bodied male peasants between the ages of 18 and 30 were forced into joining the movement under threat of being fined, expelled from their lineage, deprived of tenancy rights, or imprisoned.

A similar picture emerges from the results of field work in Hua county, home of one of the largest Red Spear contingents in Honan province. There the Red Spears were founded in the fall of 1926 by a local landlord as protection against the extortions of the Feng Army warlords. Rather than continue to remit exhorbitant amounts of silver to the rapacious warlords, this opium-addicted landlord provided money to hire a boxing teacher and purchase weapons to outfit a Red Spear unit. The movement rapidly expanded to number thousands of members in dozens of neighboring villages. According to Chinese researchers, the Red Spear leaders of Hua county — most of whom were landlords, rich peasants or local strongmen — knew that the invulnerability myth was a hoax. Hence they led their followers on a number of forays to seize weapons from the Feng Army.[22]

Although the image of a movement led by and for rural powerholders certainly emerges as the dominant one, this general impression is tempered by regional variation. Baba Takeshi has developed a differentiated picture of the Red Spears in Honan, proposing that types of Red Spear societies varied along with differences in cropping and landholding patterns. Southern Honan, known for productive wet-rice cultivation and high rates of tenancy, saw landlord-dominated Red Spear associations. Northern Honan, with a less productive agriculture based upon wheat, maize, and beans, was the home of more egalitarian Red Spear groups in which the leaders — often peasants themselves — were treated as brothers. Western Honan, its poor soil famous as a breeding ground for bandits, saw the development of Red Spear units comprised of demobilized soldiers, brigands, and local bullies. Baba notes that although poor and middle peasants constituted the main force of all Red Spear organizations, regional variations in leadership contributed to different patterns of Red Spear activity in different parts of the province.[23]

What was the relationship between the social composition of the Red Spears and their religious beliefs? Did Red Spear mentality reflect the often conservative interests of landlord-local strongmen leaders, or did it express the dynamic dreams of its rank-and-file peasant followers? Baba Takeshi suggests that the rituals which Red Spears practiced to induce invulnerability served to transcend the limitations of everyday village life. He points to the proscriptions against new initiates having sexual contact with women as evidence that the husband-wife relationship — the heart of the family bond — was temporarily severed in favor of consummating a new religious identification. Baba may well be correct in stressing the possibilities for a new style of peasant identity and activism encouraged by Red Spear injunctions. On the other hand, it also seems possible that the taboo against contact with women reflected the Confucian outlook of landlord-gentry leaders who saw no positive role for female participation. Certainly the exclusively male orientation of the Red Spears stands in marked contrast to traditional White Lotus sects, in which women played important roles as participants and teachers. In any event, as Baba emphasizes, Red Spear beliefs did not provide the basis for an attack upon landlord-gentry hegemony.[24] It seems plausible that the Red Spears' antipathy toward women, as well as their effort to restore a "moral economy" in which only the old land tax was seen as a legitimate requisition, represented the views of the rural elite more than those of poor peasants.

It is also important to keep in mind that a belief in magic was not the monopoly of the peasantry. Tai Hsüan-chih describes government troops as using their own magical potions (e.g., dog's blood) to break the power of Red Spear charms. This recalls the Wang Lun Rebellion of the eighteenth century when, as Naquin has documented, the Ch'ing soldiers also resorted to magical antidotes against rebel invulnerability rituals.[25] Thus to suggest that Red Spear reliance on "heterodox" religious rites reflected a dynamic "Little Tradition" in opposition to state orthodoxy runs the risk of drawing a sharper distinction between the beliefs of officials and peasants than probably existed in rural China, whether in the eighteenth or twentieth centuries.

Relationship to Revolution

If the Red Spears were motivated by age-old popular "superstitious" beliefs, how progressive a role could the movement play in the revolutionary upheavals of the twentieth century? As Professor Tai makes clear, would-be revolutionaries were far more interested in the Red Spears than the Red Spears were in them. Beginning in 1925, Comintern-sponsored attempts to mobilize the Red Spears were undertaken in north and central China. Occasionally the prospect of financial and military assistance struck a responsive chord, but as Tai concludes "generally speaking, Soviet incitement of the Red Spears cannot be considered successful." Time and again, the revolutionaries were rebuffed by parochially-oriented Red Spear associations. Tai notes that the Communists' lack of success in developing a peasant movement in Hupei was due to powerful Red Spear opposition.

The picture which emerges from Professor Tai's account is of a localistic movement whose objectives were basically defensive. Certainly, this very defensiveness could have important political consequences. In 1925-26, as Tai shows, the Red Spears in Honan helped warlord Wu P'ei-fu expel the National Army, in hopes thereby of gaining tax relief. When Wu himself proved an exploitative overlord, however, the Red Spears in 1927 assisted the National Army in getting rid of him. By Tai Hsüan-chih's account, the foremost contribution of the Red Spears lay not in any short-lived tactical alliances with outside revolutionaries. It lay instead in the movement's heroic resistance to the Japanese. The stubbornly defensive stance of the Red Spears meant that they were a potent force for the protection of the Chinese countryside in the face of foreign invasion.

If the fact that the Red Spears were not a reliable ally for the Kuomintang creates certain problems for historians in Taiwan, the hostility of the movement toward the Communists (both before and after 1949) has been equally troublesome for historians in the People's Republic. For a time, the Red Spears were not a popular topic of scholarly inquiry in China. What little was written in the way of memoirs or fiction focused on those rare instances of Red Spear-CCP cooperation.[26] After all, to acknowledge that a "spontaneous" rural rebellion which had mobilized millions of peasants in opposition to bandits, taxes, and the Japanese had also been antagonistic toward the Communist revolution was something of an embarrassment. In just the last few years, however, scholars in China have begun to deal more frankly with the Red Spears. Although some of these recent accounts have been published only for internal circulation [nei-pu], they offer a picture of the Red Spear Society remarkably similar to that outlined by Professor Tai.

One of the first of these recent accounts of Red Spear opposition to the Communists appeared in a 1978 study of the Huang-Ma uprising, a critical episode in the founding of the Ou-Yü-Wan Soviet (along the Hupei-Honan-Anhwei border) in the mid-1920s.[27] The study was based upon reports sent from local county Party committees to Party Central, memoirs of Party members who participated in the uprising, and field investigations conducted over many years in the area. According to this authoritative account, the local Red Spear association was established in 1926 by landlords in opposition to the organization of Communist-inspired peasant associations in the area. Boxing masters were hired from Hopei and Shantung to teach the requisite martial arts techniques. At training sessions, the boxing masters held Buddhist rosaries and recited incantations while their pupils practiced with swords and spears.

After Red Spear attacks on peasant association offices elicited retaliation in the form of landlord executions, relatives of the slain landlords organized a "Protect Property Party" [Pao-ch'an-tang] on the basis of Red Spear and people's militia units. The landlord-led party proved unable to eliminate the revolutionary threat, however. Eventually the Communists succeeded in overcoming the formidable resistance and established their soviet government.[28]

This account makes clear the substantial problems which Red Spear opposition posed for the revolutionaries. At the same time, however, the Communists did try to make some accommodation with their Red Spear rivals. In the early stages of the battle, Communist cadres "made use of old-style Red Spear organizational forms" to establish three "revolutionary Red Spear units" to fight against the landlords' forces.[29] As Mitani has aptly noted, for Communist cadres to lead the masses toward revolution meant breaking through the fetters of popular "tradition"; but this breakthrough itself often required the power of "traditional" beliefs.[30] And in the end, after the Communists staged a decisive victory in November 1927, poor peasant members of the defeated Red Spears broke with their leaders and sent more than thirty emissaries to Huang-an to seek a truce with the revolutionaries.[31]

Further discussion of Red Spear hostilities during the Huang-Ma uprising appeared in a 1980 issue of the *Cheng-chou University*

Journal. This account makes clear that the Red Spears became especially active after the split between the KMT and CCP in the spring of 1927. A formidable power in the Hupei-Honan border region, the Red Spears assisted KMT troops in "mop-up" campaigns against the peasant associations and peasant self-defense army which had been established under the direction of Tung Pi-wu. This account also acknowledges that Communist cadres, from the winter of 1926 to the spring of 1927, had used the familiar name of "red schools" (a term for Red Spear associations) to set up several units which were actually directed by the CCP. At that time, however, they made strenuous efforts to destroy the peasants' faith in Red Spear religious rituals. An especially effective method of undermining such beliefs was for the Red Army's best marksmen to take aim at Red Spear leaders. This visible disconfirmation of the invulnerability cult, combined with the patient educational efforts of Communist cadres sent to infiltrate hostile Red Spear groups, was credited with helping to win the allegiance of many rank and file Red Spear followers.[32]

A detailed discussion of Red Spear activities in Hua county, Honan—published for internal circulation in 1980—offers further evidence of the problems for revolutionary mobilization posed by local Red Spears. Although the Red Spears in Hua county began in opposition to warlord exactions, they came in time to operate as an instrument of warlord ambitions. Having experienced the agony of several Red Spear assaults, Feng Army leaders decided to turn the tables on their former enemy. They commissioned a Red Spear leader in Shantung (who was also the uncle of one of the warlord officers) to remake the Red Spears of Hua county into a friendly ally. An opium addict and former military official under the Ch'ing, this Red Spear teacher proved extraordinarily adept at remolding the Hua Red Spears—thanks in no small measure to the fact that a major Red Spear leader in Hua county had once served as his disciple. Although prominent KMT supporters in the area attempted to win over the Red Spears by providing lavish banquets in the county seat, the Feng Army's provision of guns, bullets, uniforms, and horses proved more persuasive. With the prompting of Feng Army warlords, the Red Spears launched a full-scale attack on the county seat. Only in the spring of 1928, when a vice-commander in the KMT army was sent home to his native Hua county, were many rank-and-file Red Spears persuaded to hand over their guns.[33]

As these narratives suggest, the Red Spears—albeit a formidable force for local protection—were not natural revolutionaries. Depending on the nature of available outside allies, they could as easily turn toward counter-revolutionaries (e.g., the Feng Army) as toward revolution, whether of the Kuomintang or Communist variety.

When the KMT became less of a force for change in the Chinese countryside, an accommodation with the Red Spears grew less problematic. Indeed, reports of Red Spear alliances with the KMT became increasingly common in the 1930s and 1940s. Even the Communists found it easier to cooperate with Red Spear units during the War of Resistance period.[34] But Red Spear support was notoriously unreliable, as events of the 1940s and early 1950s would demonstrate.[35]

Conclusion

Scholarship on the Red Spears has come some distance since Tai Hsüan-chih published his pioneering study. While this recent work suggests elaborations and qualifications to some of Tai's arguments, on the whole his book has stood the test of time very well. However, as I am sure Professor Tai would agree, many unanswered questions about the Red Spear Society—from its origins to its demise—remain. Let us hope that scholars will push ahead with the necessary field and documentary research so that one day we may be better able to do justice to this important chapter in modern Chinese history.

Translator's Introduction
Ronald Suleski

Among both rural peasants and local officials, the Red Spears Society has been widely known in China since the 1920s. Using information gained from meticulous research, Professor Tai Hsüan-chih has attempted to outline the origins and organization of the society. His studies have shown that no single group can be identified as *the* Red Spears, and no single form of organization characterized the groups that used the name.

Because so many elements of Chinese popular and rural cultures were incorporated into the Red Spears, a society might appear anywhere and any secret society could call itself a Red Spears group. All that was needed to found such a society were reasons to form it, the organizational resources to do so, and a name. The dangers faced by a community due to the breakdown of effective local government generally provided reason enough and existing local groups supplied the necessary organizational resources. The name frequently seemed to emerge from popular local usage or an unspoken consensus; it was not, in fact, an important aspect of the secret society. That is why there were so many groups, with different names and practicing a variety of rituals, which Tai identifies as Red-Spears-type organizations.

It was important to have a name because it helped marshall the energies of the peasants in organizing and maintaining the groups, and it fostered a certain *esprit de corps* among the members as they engaged in the serious business of the society. Believing that the chanting of magic slogans and the use of weapons decorated in distinctive colors gave them power, secret-society members sometimes defeated the armed forces of local officials, and even overcame the defenses of county seats to claim authority for themselves. After such victories, a mixture of fear and respect would sweep the surrounding countryside. The name of the society would quickly become part of local legend and its exploits would be recorded in the next edition of the local gazetteer.

In the long run the secret societies were no match for well-organzied military forces or for a trained government bureaucracy, but they could, and frequently did, capture a county seat or halt government troops marching through the countryside. Once in control, however, they seldom followed their initial military and psychological successes with effective administrative or economic control. Their victories over organized government or military authority were always temporary.

Secret societies like the Red Spears emerged in response to the pressures of daily life and the beliefs and attitudes of the peasant population. They acted spontaneously, so no group outside of the local popular culture, be it the provincial government or a more broadly based political entity, could direct the energies of the secret societies for any length of time. All the political groups in modern China, including the central government in Peking, provincial warlords, the Kuomintang, and the Communist Party, tried to manipulate the secret societies, and all of them failed.

The only individuals who successfully maintained control over a secret society for as long as three to five years were locally known and respected men. These were given such titles as "great master" [ta-fa-shih] by the society members.

The twentieth century brought new methods of warfare to China and changed the way war was fought. Since it was a time of political turmoil, all of China's legitimate and illegitimate armies quickly adopted machine guns, telegraph communications, railroads for troop transport, and, when they could, airplanes. This might have increased the effectiveness and power of the secret societies, but available records indicate that these groups never adopted the modern tools of war. The faith of secret-society members lay, not in machinery, but in individual discipline combined with magical powers obtained through the guidance of a teacher. Their weapons and tactics remained unchanged from those of centuries before. Thus, in their development and behavior the groups Tai describes are very much like other secret societies in Chinese history. However, Tai's research provides more detailed information about the Red Spears and its activities than was usually found in earlier historical accounts.

Tai Hsüan-chih was born in 1922 in Hsin-tsai hsien, Honan province, into a family which owned about four hundred mou of land near the Hsin-tsai county seat. His father was the clan elder who counseled clan members and every spring supervised the distribution of free food to members in financial trouble.

Tai experienced personally the conditions which led to the formation of secret societies and the way in which they were organized. Before Tai's birth and during his childhood, bandits flourished in the vicinity of his family's home. In 1912 and 1913 local warfare around Tai's home became serious. Although the family employed armed bodyguards, Tai's older brother, then four years old, was twice captured by bandits and had to be ransomed. When Tai was an infant, he and his mother were taken hostage by bandits and held for ten days. The most serious encounter occurred in August 1926 when bandits stormed the Hsin-tsai county seat and captured most of the males in the family, including the five-year-old Tai, his father, and an eleven-year-old brother. After about a week Tai's brother was released and told to return to the family home to secure cash for the ransom of his father. Tai was also released by the bandits. After a month in captivity, Tai's father managed to escape and rejoin his family.

In the spring of 1927, another Tai relative was captured and apparently killed by bandits who demanded money and opium. His body was never found. To avenge this murder Tai's father organized the Yellow Spears Society [Huang-ch'iang-hui], which resembled the Red Spears. A large room in one wing of the family house, where Tai and his brothers and sisters used to study, was designated as the meeting room [hui-t'ang] of the society. A man known as Teacher Liang was invited to erect an altar in this room and prepare the written magic phrases. About sixty young men joined. Members gathered in the meeting room every evening after supper to practice with broadswords and perform many of the ritual training exercises described in Tai's book. Tai, then a boy of six, would peer in the windows of the meeting room, observing the training of the society members.

Since his father was a graduate of a private academy in K'ai-feng, Tai has always felt that he did not personally believe in the power of magic incantations, but organized the Yellow Study Society so that clan members could protect themselves and their property from bandits. His father funded the society, but never took part in its rituals. It was formally disbanded in 1929 when the family left the countryside where they had been living since 1926 and returned to the Hsin-tsai county seat.

Tai has had a distinguished career as a historian. He graduated from National Hsi-pei [Northwestern] University in 1947, and taught at Taiwan National University from 1949 to 1969. He taught in the History Department of Nan-yang University in Singapore from 1969 to 1979, and served as chairman of the department from 1975 to 1977. He has been a visiting professor at National Ching-chi University in Taiwan since 1979.

Most of Tai's academic career has been devoted to studying the origins of secret socieites in modern China. Of the twenty-one articles he published between 1959 and 1978, the majority dealt with the White Lotus Society [Pai-lien-chiao] and the Heaven and Earth Society [T'ien-ti-hui]. His extensive work on the origins of the Boxer Movement resulted in the book *Research on the Boxers*. His book on the Red Spears, translated here, is entitled *The Red Spears, 1916-49*.

When reconstructing events in the history of the secret societies, Tai has been rigorous in his search for acceptable documentation. His research, in *The Red Spears* and elsewhere, is firmly based on a thorough investigation of local gazetteers and government records. He considers these the most reliable sources, their authors the most prone to seek out and report accurate factual information. He also realizes that a topic like the Red Spears demands documentation from additional sources, such as newspapers and personal accounts, and turns to those sources to supplement the official records.

My strongest criticism of *The Red Spears* is that although Tai deliberately declines to generalize about the role of secret societies in modern China, he also seems unsure of his evaluation of the role of the Red Spears within rural Chinese society. On the one hand he concludes that secret-society members were legitimately and effectively protesting corrupt officials and rapacious warlords. On the other hand he describes these people as ignorant and easily fooled by any smooth-talking and even slightly charismatic leader. He often discusses the unbearable conditions under which peasants struggled to survive, yet he seems to accept the view of many contemporary officials that the secret societies were composed of riff-raff and near-bandits living vagabond lives.

Certainly the society members were all these things, and perhaps we should thank Tai for refusing to accept a single analytical line merely for the sake of interpretive consistency. There is a difference, however, between a poor peasant forced to beg and a local bully who joins a secret society for the gang protection it affords him. To describe the peasants as ignorant and easily manipulated ignores the fact that within the context of rural life the secret society and its magic rituals provided a fairly effective means of organizing a supravillage group to deal with pressing problems. I sometimes felt in reading *The Red Spears* that Tai simply copied standard phrases from the old government reports without determining whether they truly expressed his sentiments.

These problems will not be apparent to the readers of this translation. The original Chinese-language version is written in a style which most non-native speakers of Chinese would find difficult to understand. Tai writes in a combination of early colloquial [pai-hua] and semi-classical newspaper prose. It is replete with short phrases that are better read for the general feeling they convey than for their literal meaning. In translating the book, I have usually avoided strongly literal translations in favor of natural-sounding English sentences which provide the content of the original and often use the same words, but could never be translated back into Tai's original Chinese.

A similar approach has been used in organizing paragraphs and in deciding which sections of the book to translate. Some sections contain so many names of places and individuals that they would greatly burden any English text, while not giving useful information to the typical reader of the translation. Further, in many cases a large number of similar incidents are illustrated to help Tai make his point, and general points in one chapter may be repeated in following chapters for the sake of continuity. Since these aspects detract from the organization demanded by a good English text, some sections of the book have been summarized rather than translated, and a few have been omitted altogether. The chapter and section headings used in the translation correspond to those in the original, which should help any reader who wants to compare the two.

Professor Tai sent me a copy of *The Red Spears* in 1973, shortly after it was published. I was working at the Japan Foundation in Tokyo and, after reading parts of the book, decided to prepare a summary translation. The bulk of the translation was accomplished between 1976 and 1978, when I was teaching at the University of Texas at Arlington. I was fortunate to have the assistance of two native speakers of Chinese who prepared the original translation of some portions of the book. Ms. Chang Yi-Yüan made the initial translations of chapter 1 and portions of chapter 2, and Mr. Lau Yue-ding made a draft translation of portions of chapter 2. After the translation was completed, it was checked against the original by Mr. Shi Yong in Peking during the summer of 1980. The final version was prepared in Tokyo in 1982.

Preface
T'ao Hsi-sheng

In this book,[1] T'ai Hsüan-chih explores the role of the Red Spears secret society in the complex period between the 1911 Revolution and the Northern Expedition of 1928, and the ways in which the Red Spears were involved in the social and political problems caused by the warlords and the constant warfare which plagued China at the time. This historical period is too often neglected.

In the early Republican period such self-defense organizations as the Red Spears were largest and most numerous in Honan province. Before the 1911 Revolution I travelled with my parents throughout Honan, including the cities of Lo-yang and K'ai-feng, where I lived while a middle-school student. After the 1911 Revolution, I often visited Hsin-yang. My travels gave me the opportunity to become well acquainted with the social and political conditions of north China through personal observation. There are several stories I can recall about local self-defense groups such as the Red Spears.

The area where the provinces of Honan, Anhwei, and Shantung meet, where as a boy I once travelled with my father, is notorious for bandits who shot whistling arrows to announce their coming. Although the common people there armed themselves for self-protection, they did not lightly oppose these bandits. Usually the police could not capture the highwaymen because they lacked information about their movements. Even if they managed to capture a well-known bandit leader, the leader might make a confession, or deny everything, but would never involve other members of the band or implicate those who helped him.

Southwestern Honan is mountainous and at that time was another area filled with bandits. At the end of the Ch'ing dynasty the highwaymen had strict codes of conduct among themselves. In one case, when a girl was raped the leader sentenced the responsible band member to public execution and all the members took this as a warning. One year, when I was a middle-school student returning to

K'ai-feng from a summer vacation, our carriage passed through an area where the bandits came and went freely and the common people had built fortifications and earthworks to protect themselves. This brought to mind stories of similar situations in China's past. The memory is still fresh in my mind.

To the south of the Lo River in Lo-yang hsien a road once ran into the mountains. At the end of the Ch'ing dynasty this was an area where the bandits and common people often confronted one another. In nearby regions, at the end of the Ch'ing, one could still travel to visit the temples there, but by the beginning of the Republic even the beautiful Ch'ien-ch'i Temple was used as a bandit headquarters.

Most of the men who lived in the village on the plain practiced the martial arts. My middle school in Honan was one of the first in the province and so it was well known. Behind the school was a large athletic field where, in addition to gymnastics, the students practiced the martial arts. I remember the most skillful students, two brothers who came from Lin-hsien and an uncle and his nephew from Sui-p'ing. In Lin-hsien every March a large competition in the martial arts was held just outside the city in which most of the youth participated. The best participants would dress as well-known heroes from Chinese history such as Chang Fei, Kuan-kung, and others. In Sui-p'ing hsien, people often encouraged their sons to train in the martial arts. They even employed teachers to instruct them, which accounted for their expertise. Young girls would stand at the edge of the field watching the competition and if they found a boy they liked they would seek out the head of his house to see about a marriage. My classmates at the middle school were some of these skillful boys from Lin-hsien and Sui-p'ing hsien.

The above remarks give an impression of the lives of the people in Honan at the end of the Ch'ing dynasty, but with the beginning of the Republic many political and social changes took place. During the late Ch'ing, the people of the plains encouraged their children to study the martial arts as an aid in protecting their villages. They did not believe in the use of magic practices like amulets and rituals as a means of protection. For example, when my father was working in Yeh-hsien there was a self-defense group which practiced a form of martial arts which they said could be mastered in eighteen days. My father would use his head as a weapon, hitting it against a brick without suffering any injury. He also claimed not to fear bullets, though he dared not face these "steel balls without smoke." Later, when I was in Lo-yang, I saw secret society members who did use magic charms to protect themselves. By the end of the Ch'ing many villages had earthen walls and other means of defense, but after the beginning of the Republic these were no longer sufficient. With the coming of the warlords and the increase in banditry, society became even more unstable and fighting was so widespread that it could occur anywhere. At the same time the common people reverted to belief in magic, probably because they had no other means of protection.

At the end of the Ch'ing period the bandits usually practiced a code of honor among themselves. This was because the suppression of such rebellions as the T'ai-ping Heavenly Kingdom [1851-64] left provincial and county governors with plenary powers to impose sanctions upon bandits. At that time, provincial governors could deploy troops and local officials could even order executions. Long ago China did not have a police force because villagers organized for their own defense and local authorities supported the people by granting legal permission to carry out death sentences. If bandit groups became so strong that the people and the authorities could not subdue them, regular army forces were summoned. When this occurred, the local people sometimes suffered as much as the bandits at the hands of the government troops. Thus, villagers with martial skills assisted local authorities. But, if they could not overcome the bandits they often struck a bargain with them. In such cases the bandits would agree to cease operations in the immediate vincinity and in return the people would not organize against them.

In the early 1900s, I observed local officials who were appointed to posts in the countryside under orders to eliminate banditry. They considered themselves responsible only for chasing the bandits out of their *hsien* and sometimes they resorted to negotiation to accomplish this task. Knowing that their reputations would be enhanced if the bandits left the *hsien*, they would agree to refrain from punitive action if the gangs would abandon the area. In such a case they protected their own territory by moving the brigands into a neighboring jurisdiction.

With the beginning of the Republic conditions deteriorated greatly due to the imposition of special taxes, the spread of warlordism, and so on. Local officials did not protect the people and people could not protect themselves. Bandits were everywhere. They even invaded the towns and killed officials. Obviously these authorities could not protect themselves, let alone protect the people, and the army protected no one. The warlords had no morality and the bandits no code of conduct. Where was order to come from?

Once in the late Ch'ing a bandit known as White Wolf was captured, but the government released him with only a light punishment. In the early Republic this man became the leader of a bandit gang. Whenever the gang marched, White Wolf would lock himself in a covered sedan chair and give the key to his followers to show that he had no intention of abandoning his comrades.

The roving bandit gangs were broad-based organizations but it is inappropriate to speak of them as heroes or romantic adventurers. To protect themselves the common people formed their own broad-based organizations. These groups arose partly as a reaction to rampant warlordism and partly as a response to the depredations of the bandits. The Red Spears was this sort of popular self-defense group.

In this book Tai Hsüan-chih has provided an overview and analysis of the Red Spears and their organization, and the social and political environment which spawned them. The recollections from my youth are intended as an added, more personal glimpse of the Red Spears.

Chapter I: Origins of the Red Spears

Section 1: Rise of the Village Militia

The Red Spears can be considered the legitimate offspring of the Boxer Movement and the heirs of China's village militia, so any investigation of them must begin with a consideration of the village self-defense groups. Regulations establishing the *pao-chia* system of mutual protection and responsibility first appeared in the Northern Sung period [960-1126 A.D.]. These regulations, which marked the beginning of legal recognition of organized self-defense units, permitted adult men to keep weapons such as bows, arrows, knives, and swords in their homes and to gather to practice the martial arts.[1] Regulation of self-defense forces was strictly enforced in the early Ch'ing dynasty [mid-1600s to early 1700s], when a tablet was placed on the door of every peasant home listing the name of the household head and the number of adult men dwelling there.

Based on units of ten, the *pao-chia* system formed every ten households into a *p'ai* [shield] with a headman [*t'ou*], every ten shields into a *chia* [armor] with a chief [*chang*], and every ten armor units into a *pao* [protector] with a commander [*cheng*]. The leaders of each unit were chosen from among locally prominent families, and the *pao-chia* organization was the basic method of maintaining law and order in the local areas.

During the T'ai-p'ing Rebellion of the 1850s and 1860s, the T'ai-p'ing troops captured most of south China, sending tremors of fear through north China where the imperial court was located. In encouraging local citizens to strengthen their self-defense organizations, the imperial court issued a regulation regarding the building of forts and walls as a protection against the T'ai-p'ings. The regulation stated,

> The best way to meet the current problem is to encourage local people to build a number of forts, each consisting of ten or more villages, or even

1

several score of villages. When a threat is posed by
bandits, the people can alternate manning the walls,
and when the bandits are absent the people will be
free to go about their ordinary business, farming and
protecting their families individually. This network of
forts would give the people courage to defend themselves against the bandits. Two or three civil officials,
military officers, and several members of the local
gentry would be assigned to each fort to supervise its
defensive activities. Regardless of where the bandits
strike, it would be difficult for them to break through
the defensive network because the deep ditches and
strong walls would be everywhere. Moreover, the
people would not be captured by the bandits and their
grain, domestic animals, and poultry would be safe.
Encouraging powerful militia would progressively
reduce the numbers of bandits.[2]

The imperial court also adopted a proposal submitted by Kung
Ching-han, a commissioner for border affairs, which contained
further details on the best way to meet the threat posed by the
T'ai-p'ings. It suggested,

that officials travel in the countryside, encouraging
local people to organize for self-defense and build
forts; that through administrative reorganization
some small villages be annexed to larger ones; and
that present defensive positions in exposed areas be
relocated to more easily defensible territory. When
there are no bandits, the people can go about their
farming and trading in a peaceful manner. When
bandits approach, the people can close the gates and
man the towers, defending the forts together. The
government could provide a unit of two or three
thousand soldiers. Such a force would not have to
meet the bandits head on, but could pursue the
enemies from the rear or cut them off in front. If the
bandits attack a fort troops would be sent to relieve
the people within, and if the bandits begin to
withdraw the troops would pursue them.[3]

In February 1853, Li Hui, governor of Shantung province, ordered local citizens to organize self-defense units, to strengthen defensive earth-works, and to clear flat ground to provide unobstructed fields of vision. Several high officials were appointed by the imperial government to oversee the creation and management of this militia. These included Li Hsiang-fen, former viceroy for the transportation of tribute rice; Feng Te-hsing, former governor of Hunan province; and T'ien Tsai-t'ien, a number of the imperial guard. Further, the Ch'ing court approved the appointment of certain officials to manage local militias in their areas.

Governor Li Hui urged the people of each locality to develop a specific strategy for meeting the threat of the T'ai-p'ings. He feared that policies imposed from above might lead to corruption and irregularities at the local level. He wrote to the emperor,

> Because of the different circumstances among the provinces, each area should develop its own program for training militia so that these local forces will be accepted by the people. Parts of Shantung province, because they have major roads or are near Honan and Kiangsu, where the T'ai-p'ings are concentrated, are ravaged by bandits. Other districts have remained peaceful, so there is no need to form militia there. To do so would waste the people's time, interrupt their work, and needlessly upset local activities. My personal suggestion is to deal separately with the issues of annexing villages and militia training. Some areas could unite for better protection, but do not necessarily have to form militia now. In other places it is not only necessary to unite, but the people should be ordered to learn drill and to use basic military techniques. In some areas banditry is so widespread that other districts will probably prefer not to make cooperative arrangements with them. In fact, annexing such districts might force some of the local population into banditry. It would be better in those places to form local militia only and not unite them with other districts.[4]

The emperor agreed with Governor Li's proposal and adopted it as the guideline for action.

Li Hui apparently feared that local officials could not effectively explain the regulations and organize the militia, and that people would not accept the plan if the units were organized by government clerks. He felt the plan would fare better if locally prominent and respected gentry served as a bridge between the common people and government officials by advocating and implementing the scheme. This would enable the government to achieve twice as much with half the effort. He located eight fairly high-ranking officials who were on leave from government service and residing at their homes in Shantung province, and ordered them to organize the local militia. Among these men were Fu Sheng-hsün, former governor of Kiangsu province; a former vice-minister of public works; and a former provincial treasurer of Honan province. Various county magistrates were sent to low-level administrative districts to explain the new rules to the local gentry and the common people. They were asked to maintain high public visibility and to establish contact with as many citizens as possible. Li then gave overall responsibility for supervision of this operation to Tao-tai Li En-kuang and Expectant Tao-tai Liu Ching-k'ai.[5]

Because the province had been stable for some time, the scheme met with very little active cooperation. Most civil officials did not understand military needs, and the people could not imagine having to abandon their homes because of fighting. Wealthy families were unwilling to contribute funds, and the poor were afraid of losing their jobs. So, although the plan was advocated by many officials, the people would not participate.

A detailed progress report on the organization of local militia was sent to the emperor by Mao Hung-pin, one of the officials in charge of the project. His report stated,

> Having received the order from the emperor, I returned to my hometown to organize the local militia. As I understand it, the idea of maintaining militia in local areas began with the system of quartering troops in the homes of villagers. Such a system could never be implemented today, partly because customs have changed since ancient times and partly due to the current attitudes of the people. The country has been at peace for so long that people have almost forgotten that war exists. They live comfortably, happily, and safely, and if anything untoward happened they would not know how to deal

with it. My region is located at the confluence of several jurisdictions, and the people feel no responsibility for the situation in surrounding areas; this makes my task even more difficult and complicated.

Although we have vigorously promoted the present plan, people are wary of it and doubt its necessity. If someone attempts to carry out our suggestions, the majority criticize him. Despite hardships and criticism, my staff and I have tried to implement the project. First, we drafted and announced the regulations. We visited each *hsien* in search of upright and prominent people to undertake the leadership of local militia units. We taught these men to annex villages by redistricting, to provide for mutual defense, and asked them to encourage their people to build forts and dig trenches. We established eight bureaus to instruct the people in military drill and supplied them with food. We organized a corps of militia composed of the strongest men, one that could mobilize quickly in response to a threat. Finally, when people began to understand the concept of mutual defense, they no longer considered military training unbearable.

In the area surrounding the capital of Shantung province there are 8 districts, 239 roads, and 803 villages. The Ta-ch'ing River, which is 40 *li* from the western edge of the city, is the main access to the city for those who come from the west. Initially I worked with the acting county magistrate, Wang Yen-shan, to strengthen military forces in the outlying areas and we organized one corps to serve 54 villages. Then we established local militia in a number of these villages. Other existing units draw from several score or 100 or more villages. There are more than 600 villages in my jurisdiction and more than 300 *li* that can be considered strategic. Some more secluded areas have also formed militia units.

Since the court has lent its prestige to this plan, its impact on the people is bound to be considerable. For example, on one occasion the officials of Ts'ao-hsien thought the T'ai-p'ing bandits from Kuang-tung would cross the Yellow River so, in spite

of heavy rain, we went to that city and assembled all
the militia units there. The populace was encouraged
by the common spirit of hostility toward the bandits.
The people were loyal and brave, inspired by the
excellent directions of the militia commanders. I beg
Your Majesty to allow me to reward them
appropriately. This report was written by P'eng
Yi-chu and Li Hung-ch'ou.[6]

Mao's request was approved, and the local gentry and common
people were rewarded by the imperial court.

With recognition from the court, enthusiasm for the
establishment of local militia spread, and many units were created
voluntarily. Many local officials willingly participated in the scheme,
although some remained in seclusion and left the creation of militia
solely in the hands of gentry leaders and the common people. In
September 1853, Mao Hung-pin dispatched a second report to the
throne, asking that eight more officials be added to those responsible
for military training. Again, eight well-known officials who were
then residing at their homes throughout Shantung were assigned to
the project. When the new governor, Chang Liang-chi, assumed his
post in Shantung in October 1853, he published the regulations
concerning the annexation of villages and ordered all magistrates in
the hsien to carry them out.

The defensive measures taken in Shantung were not in vain. In
February 1854, the northernmost units of the T'ai-p'ing army
entered the province. Although the new governor was ordered to
defend the province, the T'ai-p'ings managed to occupy six Shantung
counties in succession. They quickly filled provincial posts with their
own men and established administrative offices. By late April,
however, they began to retreat. Lacking food for their army, they
abandoned Lin-chin by 22 April, and Kuan-hsien six days later,
fleeing to the south. During their withdrawal they were intercepted
and often defeated by local militia units. Some militia commanders,
including Huang Sheng-ts'ai and Tseng Li-ch'ang, died in the
fighting.[7] Several hundred gentry and common citizens received
promotions or commendations from the emperor as a result of the
victories over the T'ai-p'ing forces. These heros were highly
acclaimed and soon militia units began forming all over the province.
Each unit chose a name, for example, Respect for Righteousness
[Shang-i] and Righteous Inclination [Hao-i].[8] Some hsien had as few
as four and others as many as several score militia units.

With the popularity of the militia came increased status for their leaders. Each local unit had a head [*t'uan-chang*] who supervised the militia in his home village and sometimes in as many as four others nearby. The extent of his influence depended on his ability and power.[9]

Occasionally, of course, there were militia leaders who worked, not for the good of the nation, but for personal gain. These men used their official authority for private profit, practiced unethical methods, and greedily took bribes. They often acted arbitrarily in deciding village affairs, and would free prisoners or execute them on a whim. Local officials sometimes asked militia leaders to capture criminals or pursue bandits, and soon the people came to fear their militia leader more than the government officials. The power of the militia leaders was soon boundless and it became necessary to bring them under control. By May 1855 it was clear that the northern advance of the T'ai-p'ings had been halted, and officials in Shantung moved to reduce the strength of the local militia. The governor ordered the militia of all districts and *hsien* to relinquish their arms and return their members to full-time agricultural work. When the units disbanded, the spirit of motivation behind the local militia in Shantung disintegrated.

Section 2: Transformation of the Village Militia

In the mid-1800s village militia in north China maintained a defense of local areas against antigovernment forces, or "bandits," as they were termed by government officials. In 1856, the Nien rebels entered Shantung province, but they met with stiff resistance from militia units. So effective were their actions that the provincial governor asked the emperor to bestow an official rank on the head of the village militia in Chun City, and he was appointed an assistant *hsien* magistrate. Other officials connected with the village militia also were rewarded by the court.

Despite this, as time went on, local units began to act independently. Sometimes they even used the power granted to them by the government to circumvent its laws. This happened in Shantung, where militia weapons were sometimes used in incidents arising from personal vendettas or feuds. Even during times of peace, when local authority was strong, many such incidents occurred. As a result, when the idea of strengthening local militia was periodically raised, some felt that " . . . to train local militia openly and gather hundreds of strong young men together in the same place is to build a force that cannot be controlled."[10]

To prevent the village from acting outside its authority, in March 1860 the emperor ordered Tu Chiao, a vice-minister in the Ministry of Finance then residing in Shantung, to supervise local units. Tu Chiao established a special bureau in the province and published regulations concerning the command structure, symbols, and rules governing local militia. He also ordered the *hsien* magistrates and the provincial governor to give special authority to the militia heads, powers with which provincial officials were not to interfere. The militia leaders and county magistrates now found themselves in competing positions.

As a result, the village militia changed radically, and these small-scale defensive units under official supervision became centers of local power in which the militia leader assumed many prerogatives. Often these leaders became arrogant and uncontrollable. In some areas " . . . the leaders of the village militia were so proud of the way their units had defeated the Nien rebels that they began to treat the local inhabitants as if they were their subjects. They released or killed people as they wished, and collected money without restraint. In time they became so powerful that an order by a local government official was not as effective as a word from the head of the village militia."[11] In one case a man named Han Chih-nan, under the pretext of training village militia, levied a tax based on the amount of each farmer's land. He also organized the people to resist government taxes. When a citizen named Wang Hsing-pang paid taxes to the government, his house was burned down.

A number of other examples of local militia units acting against official government authority have been recorded. In one instance, militia leaders in the P'ing-yüan area gathered several thousand local members and surrounded the town, firing on it throughout the night. They declared that persons who paid taxes to the government in lieu of joining their protest would see their houses burned and then would be killed. When the *hsien* magistrate proved unable to control the militia, their illegal actions increased. The problem was solved only when regular troops were brought in at the request of the magistrate.

In other areas, such as Chih-hsien, militia leaders in command of nearly one thousand men joined local bandits, like Yen Yü-hui and others, who had over five hundred men, and attacked the county seat. They claimed their purpose was to force the *hsien* magistrate to reduce the food tax. The magistrate led some of his men against the rebel forces. Although some of the magistrate's men were killed, and two rebel leaders seized and executed, the militia managed to enter the city and burn down the magistrate's office.

Other local officials, seeing the plight of the magistrate in Chih-hsien and his inability to control the militia, abandoned their responsibility to maintain law and order and instead tried to avoid confrontations with the local forces. Soon similar incidents occurred elsewhere in the province and other militia units began protesting high taxes. A rebel militia unit in Yüeh-ling evicted the *hsien* magistrate, captured his official seal, and began issuing documents with it. Other militia units, led by local officials, were called into action against them. Several thousand men were involved in this conflict.[12]

Local officials had trained the militia to preserve peace, but now these units were breaking the law and no one seemed able to control them. In fact, the membership of rebel militia units was growing. A report submitted by the Wu-ting magistrate, Chang Ting-fu, named eight *hsien* where various tax protests were organized by militia units and where local officials were afraid to ask for government troops. Government grain collection-areas, he reported, had been seized by the people or plundered, and citizens entering towns to pay their taxes had been attacked. Armed rebels had forcibly entered government offices in some areas. His report concluded with a call for government troops to restore order.[13] A high official was dispatched to the area to bring the troublemakers to justice, but the protests only increased.[14]

Numerous *hsien* in Shantung were likewise affected by troubles involving local militia. In Hui-min hsien, six cities were surrounded by militia and local officials could not leave. In about ten *hsien* in the Wu-ting district, commercial traffic was halted; four other *hsien* had similar problems. In Ch'ing-hsien militia officers set themselves up as officials to receive taxes from the people. Citizens of Po-p'ing hsien were greatly relieved when a powerful and oppressive militia leader, Hu Te-chün, was seized and killed by a local magistrate. When Hu's remaining troops attacked the town, burning and looting, they accused a man named Sung of Hu's illegal execution. As a result Sung was arrested by the provincial governor.[15] Thus, some militia units, with their burning, killing, and abuse of local officials, became virtual bandit gangs. Their leaders became petty tyrants. Naturally it was considered wise to disband militia units that engaged in disruptive activities.

Section 3: The Red Spears

The original purpose of the village militia was to protect homes and families, to control bandit activity, and to provide other forms of mutual assistance. Some units and united village associations[16] turned to banditry and other illegal activities, but their numbers were relatively small. The majority of the militia members were law abiding.[17]

By 1875 most of Shantung province was peaceful, but the militia units continued to train. Often, in February or March when there was no work to be done in the fields, local units would hold competitions at the regional markets.[18] If such a contest was held during the time of the early rains, the participants were called the Spring Rain Match Society [Mei-hua ch'üan-hui].

In 1887, a sectarian dispute developed among some Chinese Christians in Shantung's Kuan-hsien, and a Spring Rain Match Society took up arms against those involved. It became a sort of anti-Christian group, claiming invincibility against bullets because spirits had entered its members bodies. It adopted various ritual practices, and early in 1898 changed its name to the Boxer Society [I-ho t'uan], which, of course, precipitated the Boxer Rebellion of 1900. Although they were defeated in 1900 by Western allied forces and Ch'ing dynasty troops, few Boxers were killed. Most removed their identifying red sashes, hid their weapons, and returned to their homes in the countryside.

In 1916, after the death of Yüan Shih-k'ai, the country became politically divided. Banditry flourished once again, especially in north China; almost every day there were reports of killings and robberies.[19] After a fifteen-year hiatus, the Boxer Society was resurrected. It did not keep its old name, but called itself the Red Spears Society [Hung-ch'iang-hui].

Because the rural peasants lacked modern weapons they armed themselves with spears. A spear's tip had a sharp steel blade, and to the end of its long handle, next to the steel tip, they fastened a horse's tail which had been dyed red, a piece of cloth, or a tassel. The young people who joined the society would assemble with their spears in the society meeting hall every evening after dinner. There they would burn incense, worship the spirits, recite magic formulae, and practice with their weapons. Two members were always on guard in case of danger. In an emergency they would beat a gong or blow a horn and the members would quickly assemble, carrying their red-tasseled spears.

The society was founded in western Shantung,[20] and spread to southern Hopei, Honan, northern Kiangsu, and northern Anhwei.[21] The gazetteer for An-yang hsien records the founding of the Red Spears: "After the establishment of the Republic, the nation was unstable, bandit outrages occurred daily, and even government troops caused problems. To protect themselves, the people organized societies such as the Red Spears, the Yellow Silk Society, the White Tassels, the Green Tassels, the Heavenly Gate Society, and so on."[22] Red Spears groups were especially active in north China in 1920, when the warlords flourished, and bandits and irregular troops harassed the populace. People joined the Red Spears as a means of defense against the bandits.[23] As its membership grew, the society spread even to some southern provinces; however, it remained most active in Honan, Shantung, and Hopei.

There is a popular but mistaken notion that the Red Spears evolved from the Benevolent Righteousness Society [Jen-i-hui], which in turn had its roots in the Boxer Society.[24] A brief overview of the history of the Benevolent Righteousness Society will demonstrate the falsity of this claim.

The Benevolent Righteousness Society was founded in 1892 by Li Yüan-ching from K'ai-feng in Honan. Those who joined the society took a blood oath and vowed to live and die together. They worshipped Kuan Yün-ch'ang as their patron and called each other elder or younger brother. Divided into two large units, one under a red flag and one under a black flag, they opposed corrupt officials, aiming to overthrow the Manchu Ch'ing dynasty and restore Han [Chinese] rule to China. They formed links with other secret societies such as the Heaven and Earth Society, the Hung League [Hung-men-hui], and the Elder Brother Society [Ke-lao-hui].[25]

Their founder led them in an attack against the county seat of Ch'en-liu hsien in 1903, calling for repeal of a tax increase along the Yellow River and demanding the removal of corrupt officials. The society was dispersed by Ch'ing government troops.[26] In March 1906, following an abortive uprising in 1905,[27] the Benevolent Righteousness Society rose up in arms in Honan's Hsi-p'ing hsien. The society's leader, Miao Chin-sheng, called himself "the Heavenly King" [t'ien wang], and after drinking blood and reciting magic formulae, society members proclaimed themselves invincible against weapons. Their slogan was "Overthrow the Ch'ing and Crush the Foreigners." Several of their leaders declared themselves viceroys. The society did not engage in looting, but several *hsien* in the vicinity were apprehensive. The rebellion was finally crushed by government troops.[28] Obviously this was a branch, faction, or alias of the Heaven and Earth Society. Its origin, purpose, fabric, and rituals differed greatly from those of the Boxers and the Red Spears. We should not confuse them.

Chapter II: Modern China and the Red Spears

Section 1: Political Background

After the establishment of the Republic in 1912, local government throughout China's provinces became chaotic. In the absence of an overall unified structure, affairs at the village level were usually handled at the discretion of local officials. It was almost inevitable that under the haphazard and debased forms of local control which then developed, pure self-interest would rule the day, leading to political corruption and social unrest.[1] Warlordism added to the problem, as each commander strove to enlarge his territory and true control passed back and forth. When certain territory was occupied, its local officials became agents of the warlord, providing supplies for his army.[2]

These political and military activities had no benefit whatsoever for the people; no matter what happened, the inhabitants paid. A song in An-yang hsien recorded their feelings:

> An-yang hsien has much land which gives good grain and cotton. But, because of this turmoil, there is never enough to eat or enough to wear. The rich, how can they be happy? They fear the soldiers and officials. Forced to sell their land and their houses, their hearts are rent as if by knives. The poor also suffer and cannot live in peace. Their sons are struck down, their daughters raped, and their cottages sold. The *hsien* magistrate does not care; he is occupied with singsong girls and mah-jong. He pays no mind to the people and does not pursue the bandits; he only knows how to take money from every family.[3]

13

The people had no faith in a government that seemed only to want their money. They expressed their opinions through sayings such as "Whoever is sitting on the emperor's throne, pay him his taxes."[4]

Many peasants had a fatalistic view of the world and considered their lot ordained by fate. In the words of a popular folk song, "Some families have money but no sons, and those with sons often have less to eat and wear. Fate decrees which families shall have money and no sons, so those with sons and no money should not blame heaven. Bad is bad, good is good; common is common, precious is precious. All has been decreed and cannot be changed, so the knowing man adapts and survives. If we had one day without worries, it would be bliss."[5] Many of the peasants felt that, "Wealth and poverty are determined by fate, just as it is certain that we must live and then die."[6] Naturally the people were skeptical about officials who, in their view entered the profession only to live well—that was the nature of officials.[7] As conditions in the countryside worsened, the people felt they had no recourse to local officials. The people had sayings describing this state of affairs, for example, "The *yamen* gate is open to the rich. If you need to see an official but have no money, you cannot enter."[8] Similar sayings were, "To enter a lawsuit is as difficult as to gain salt from water";[9] and "If you must see an official, see him; after you have seen him, you'll be the poorer for it."[10]

Because the people felt their officials paid no attention to local affairs, they avoided contact with them.[11] Because local officials provided little protection, and the people could organize large units for defense, various secret societies began to emerge. Reasons for the birth of such a secret society are described in the *Gazetteer for Ch'eng-an hsien:*

> In 1920 there was a great famine in the *hsien* and when spring came there was no grain to be had. Many people died, some left for other places, some turned to banditry, and many persons were kidnapped and held for ransom. The following year there was a good cotton crop and troops of actors came to the area to celebrate, but the people were forced to pay for the extertainment. Then banditry became rife and the people could not live in peace. This was the first reason.
>
> The local officials themselves inspected the cases of attack and usually government troops were

dispatched to chase the bandits. If bandits fled beyond the range of the troops, the officials would issue a wanted circular [a general public notice for the arrest of a criminal at large]. These government methods gave some consolation to the people. Often, however, government troops did not care to pursue bandits, although they demanded provisions in the area to which they were sent. [They allowed the bandits to escape] because a local official would not issue orders to pursue them. The people knew that no one would protect them. This is the second reason.

Even though acts of brigandage increased greatly, government patrols in the area were infrequent. When peasants tried to make an official report of a robbery, they were harrassed by the local officials, who claimed the report was not detailed enough, or found other ways to discourage them. The people learned to suffer the bandit attacks without reporting them. As a result, the local authorities lost the respect of the inhabitants, who wondered whether these officials were of any use at all. This is the third reason.

Fighting between northern warlords occurred in the area in 1925. When one army retreated, another soon arrived to take its place. Often a local official sent his subordinates into the area to collect carts, food, and men, and then used these goods and laborers to ingratiate himself with the warlords. The expense of these visits was an added burden borne by the people. Whenever someone encountered an official, the officials asked for money, so the people came to regard the government as nothing more than a tax-collecting institution. Through it all, the bandits increased their numbers and their crimes against the people. This is the fourth reason.

During the summer and autumn of 1926, when another official was appointed to administer the *hsien*, fighting broke out once again. Troops were quartered in almost every home and the roads were patrolled by soldiers. Businesses ceased their commercial activities, peasants stopped working in the fields, and life in the *hsien* was at a standstill.

From October to December the new official collected taxes for 1926 and for 1927 in advance. He forced landowners to buy bonds and in those two months alone collected over three hundred thousand *yüan*. He also confiscated numberless carts, men, and supplies. Since there were insufficient policemen to control the local population, this official assigned two hundred soldiers to help the police. Meanwhile he contined to collect taxes to fund the *hsien* administration. Many families were reduced to pawning all they owned and selling their children. They were driven to despair, the bitterness penetrating their very bones. They ground their teeth with hatred for the local officials. This is the fifth reason.

For these reasons, at the beginning of 1927 a group of Red Spears, led by Liu Hsi-hsien, who was later killed, entered the *hsien* from Shantung province. Their call for opposition to illegal taxes and control of banditry stirred the populace, although people did not believe that by eating the ashes of an amulet and reciting a magic formula they could be protected against bullets. Shortly thereafter officials announced that the local warlord wanted seventy carts and thirty thousand *yüan* from the *hsien*, The peasants were unable to comply with the demand, yet they feared punishment; so, some shrewd villagers joined the Red Spears.

As people were reduced to these desperate actions, the membership of secret societies grew. Peasants joined groups called the Heaven and Earth Society, the Yellow Pebbles Society, the White Tassels, and several others. The groups were varied, but they had similar goals: controlling banditry and opposing illegal taxes.[12]

The above report demonstrates that people organized to protect themselves in the face of the breakdown of authority at the local level. Extreme political corruption was common, with local officials exploiting the people instead of protecting them. These officials took no responsibility when bandits attacked or blackmailed villagers, or when the warlords extorted money, except to flatter and ingratiate themselves with the warlords by means of the people's wealth. In

China's countryside the peasants were like unprotected lambs, subject to the vicious attacks of the warlord wolves.[13]

Section 2: Military Background

Warlordism became rampant in China shortly after the founding of the Republic, bringing with it large roving armies, constant fighting, and high taxes to pay the troops. The province of Szechuan, for example, recorded 479 battles between 1912 and 1933, an average of more than 20 battles per year.[14] Szechuan had eight armies, thirty divisions, thirty-three mixed brigades, and more than three hundred thousand troops.[15] In 1924 alone, Shansi province had three large armies which contained over two hundred thousand troops.[16]

The northeastern provinces also had many warlord forces. Shantung province had about two hundred thousand troops.[17] In 1925, Honan province had four large units stationed within its boundaries. The first was the Second Kuo-min Army, consisting of eleven divisions, eighteen mixed brigades, two cavalry brigades, twelve territorial units, and six independent infantry units, totalling over two hundred thousand troops.[18] The second large unit was the Brave Army [I-chün] of four mixed brigades and one independent unit. The third was the Honan Reconstruction Army, divided into four routes and three brigades, plus special guard and patrol units. The fourth was the Third Kuo-min Army, with two divisions, seven brigades, six mixed brigades, and three reserve brigades. There was enough manpower to form an additional three brigades and four units.[19] Thus, the number of warlord troops in the four provinces of Szechuan, Shansi, Shantung, and Honan came to over one million men; one can imagine how many troops were stationed in the other provinces as well.

Because so many men were under arms, the amount of money needed to maintain them increased regularly. For example, the central government in 1916 had a military affairs budget of 152,910,000 *yüan*. By 1928 the figure had increased to 800,000,000 *yüan*.[20] A similar situation existed in the provinces. For example, the 1925 military budget of Honan equalled the 1924 budgets of Chihli, Shantung, and Honan provinces combined.[21] Revenues collected by the central and provincial administrations were never sufficient to meet the cost of military provisions, let alone arms and ammunition. Through land taxes, debased currency, and numerous surtaxes, the peasants who provided these funds were drained.[22] The excesses of the warlords knew no bounds. To obtain more funds they issued bonds, demanded money,[23] tampered with government offices, and instituted all sorts of special levies. Local gentry and officials were constantly pressed to provide funds, and each village was threatened if it did not comply.[24]

An accounting of the supplies required by a single warlord unit in one county will serve as an illustration of the amount of goods provided by China's peasants. The following is a list of supplies requisitioned from Tung-ming hsien in Honan during a one-year period.

February 1930: The Twenty-fourth Division, consisting of 8,000 men, required 5,000 catties of flour, 5,000 catties of millet, 9,000 catties of rice straw, 1,500 catties of bran, 2,000 catties of kao-liang, and 19 large carts.

March 1930: The Army of the Fourth Flank, a force of 80,000 thousand led by Shih Yu-san, used over 5,000,000 catties of flour, over 500,000 catties of steamed bread, 356,000 catties of rice straw, 270,000 catties of bran flour, 65,000 catties of green beans, 35,000 catties of millet, 600,000 catties of kindling wood, 380,000 catties of red bean paste, and 800 large carts.

October 1930: The Pacification Army, stationed in eastern Honan, was composed of over 6,000 men. The First Brigade used 5,000 catties of flour, 5,000 catties of millet, 3,000 catties of red bean paste, 3,000 catties of black beans, 12,000 catties of grass, 10,000 catties of kindling wood, and 5,000 catties of bran. The Second Brigade used 5,000 catties of flour, 5,000 catties of millet, 3,000 catties of red bean paste, 3,000 catties of black beans, 12,000 catties of straw, 10,000 catties of kindling wood, and 5,000 catties of bran flour.

October 1930: The First Cavalry Division of the Revolutionary Army, with 6,000 men and horses, used 1,100 yüan, 2,600 catties of straw for sleeping, 15,800 catties of grass, 145,003 catties of bran flour, 22,500 catties of flour, 46,000 catties of wheat, 12,000 catties of steamed bread, 158,000 catties of firewood, and 16,900 catties of red bean paste.

December 1930: The Thirteenth Division required 15 large carts.

January 1931: One unit of the newly formed Sixth Infantry Brigade required 52,500 yüan, 238,000 catties of steamed bread, 12,000 catties of bran, 425,000 catties of kindling wood, 50,000 catties of grass, 35 large carts, and 105 horses.[25]

The people of Tung-ming hsien were pressed from all sides. In addition, during 1924 the Yellow River overflowed its banks five times, causing much suffering.[26] Another source states that in the period from February 1930 to January 1931 the people of the same *hsien* provided various armies with over 5,000,000 catties of flour, over 7,000,000 catties of steamed bread, 46,000 catties of wheat, 5,600 catties of green beans, 6,000 catties of black beans, 50,000 catties of millet, 494,900 catties of kaoliang, 442,503 catties of bran, 457,500 catties of rice straw, and 1,203,000 catties of kindling wood. The meal and flour they provided came to over 2,330,000 catties and the straw and kindling to over 1,660,500 catties. Since the population of the *hsien* at that time was 39,351 households, or 217,759 people,[27] each household provided an average of over 100 catties of supplies consisting of 60 catties of grain and 42 catties of straw and firewood. In other words, an average of 20 catties of supplies were requisitioned from each person. This figure does not include the 53,600 *yüan* or the value of the peasants' labor. Soon they did not have enough to eat themselves, and certainly nothing left to give.[28]

Similar stories could be told for other *hsien*, including Wang-tou hsien in Hopei. During the single month of July 1931, the 84,025 people of this *hsien* provided over 45,294 catties of food and 313,228 catties of kindling and straw to warlord forces. That amounted to more than 3 catties of food and 4 catties of supplies per household during the month. The poor were reduced to eating gruel. Even in good years they could ill afford to part with such quantities of food and fuel.[29]

The two examples above describe conditions in north China in the early 1930s, at the conclusion of the Northern Expedition. One can imagine that under the warlords of the 1920s conditions were even worse. Simply the large amount of money extorted implies that this was the case. For example, in 1926 warlord units in Hopei's Ching-hsien took 222,532 *yüan*.[30] Between 1930 and 1931, the warlord commander, Shih Yu-san, required over 400,000 *yüan* for his troops, which was over five times greater than normal tax levies. Troops stationed in Honan's An-yang hsien during a period of several months required over 1 million *yüan* in funds.[32]

Besides requisitioning money and supplies, the warlords imposed numerous taxes and surtaxes. When Chang Tsung-ch'ang ruled Shantung province, he imposed fifty-one such special taxes on the people.[33] As if this were not enough, other financial burdens were placed on the province as well. The provincial Bureau of Finance negotiated public loans of 563,300 *yüan* from the Bank of China and 377,000 *yüan* from the Bank of Communications. Because the provincial bank borrowed money to protect its holdings, the Bureau of Finance owed an additional 283,000 *yüan* to the Bank of China and 283,000 *yüan* to the Bank of Communications. Chang Tsung-ch'ang himself demanded 690,000 *yüan* from the Bank of China, and received a loan of 246,000 *yüan* from the Bank of Communications. Other loans from the Bank of China totalled more than 42,300 *yüan*. Among the currencies issued and circulated by provincial authorities were notes of the Bank of Shantung, military script, and gold reserve notes. The value of such notes came to at least 30,000,000 *yüan*. The notes were never backed adequately and soon became worthless.[34] Chang Tsung-ch'ang ruled Shantung from June 1925 to April 1928 (when he escaped under cover of darkness). During that time he took at least 350,000,000 *yüan* from the province.[35]

The people of Shantung had many songs and poems that expressed their hatred for Chang. Among them was a song which said, "Chang Tsung-ch'ang rules Shantung, and the people of Shantung feel his wrath. They fear neither the wind nor the rain, but only fear his soldiers." Another song went, "Governor Chang rules Shantung; he wants silver and money. He imposes taxes on chickens and dogs, and your eyes will be gouged out if you refuse to pay."[36] Other warlords such as Wu P'ei-fu, who cut down trees protecting the banks of the Yellow River in order to sell timber,[37] cared nothing for the millions of people whose lives were endangered by their actions.

Many times peasants were conscripted by warlord armies and pressed into service as carters to work with animals and wagons. Carts transported ammunition and supplies, such as kindling for cooking fires, and carters drove the carts or led the animals pulling the carts. The warlords sometimes used carters for more sinister purposes. They might be sent to the head of a column to trip land mines or be ordered to lead a burning cart into enemy lines at the head of an attack unit.[38]

Carters in the early years were usually former laborers; later, merchants, students, and even gentry were forced to perform such services.[39] Exemptions were possible, but had to be bought from the warlords. Peasants were frightened of conscription and its perils, so able-bodied men hid whenever warlord troops approached their villages and towns.[40] Some reports stated that at most half of the conscripted soldiers managed to return to their villages. It follows that the other half were sacrificed by the warlords, cannon fodder sent to their deaths in battle. Peasants expressed in song their fear of being cruelly sacrificed by irresponsible warlord officers.[41]

Many peasants and villages were caught in the middle of warlord battles.[42] Homes might be looted or completely destroyed and all food and supplies taken.[43] The only recourse for many peasants was to organize Red Spears societies and attempt to defend themselves with swords and spears. Occasionally *hsien* gazeteers, such as the one for Hsin-yang hsien, recorded in detail the sufferings of the peasants and their consequent decisions to organize into Red Spears societies.[44] Accounts such as these make it clear that the Red Spears and other secret societies were founded in direct response to the killing, looting, and other depredations of warlord troops.[45]

Section 3: Economic Background

China is truly an agricultural nation, with about 90 percent of its people engaged in farming. Although they can be distinguished in various ways, in the 1920s the majority were peasants who owned and worked small plots of land. This was the case in Hopei's Hsin-ho hsien for 99 percent of the population.[46] According to statistics recorded at the beginning of this century, each peasant owned only 3.43 *mou* of arable land.[47]

A number of factors account for the hard lives of most Chinese peasants in the early Republican period. First, a disproportionately large number of people needed the products of a limited amount of land, and the land itself was often poor. Most land in north China is dry and not very fertile, so the people there lived poor and simple lives.[48] The males worked hard in the fields while the women often wove cloth,[49] spinning, weaving, and dyeing it themselves. Those whose standard of living was below that of the middle peasant never got new clothes until the old ones could no longer be patched.[50] Their diet consisted of kaoliang, millet, and soybeans as the main staples; only 10 or 20 percent of their diet was wheat. Meats were reserved exclusively for festivals and the people normally ate their vegetarian meals without even salt or oil.[51] During the winter, 80 percent of the families often subsisted on vegetable soup.[52] They struck flints to produce fire and used cotton oil for light. Life was very difficult.

Because of the meagerness of the land, the people remained in hopeless poverty. The situation in the 1920s and mid-1930s was described in the *Gazetteer for Tung-p'ing hsien* which said,

Because of the limitations of the land and the increasing population, the produce from a years' farming is insufficient to meet the needs of the people of the *hsien*. At least 20 to 30 percent of the people have gone to Manchuria to make a living, which indicates the seriousness of the lack of food within the *hsien*. In the summer the people eat three meals a day, but in winter they eat only two. During the summer they can eat wheat, but during the other three seasons they eat mostly cereals, beans, and corn, and only a few wealthy families, institutions, or schools can provide wheat throughout the year. Most people work hard every day and still cannot afford the grain needed to raise pigs or cattle. They even eat leaves and wild vegetables such as carrots and potatoes to supplement their diet. It is common knowledge that people are suffering from the cold weather and from hunger.[53]

This situation was typical of years with a normal harvest; when a famine occurred the people resorted to the leaves of trees for food.[54]

A second cause of the hard life in north China was the high frequency of natural calamities. The number of disasters was especially high because of undeveloped methods of farming and irrigation. The most serious calamities were floods, droughts, and locusts.

Ta-ming hsien in Hopei province recorded a series of natural disasters between 1913 and 1933. For example, in the year 1913 there were strong winds in February, a flood of the Yü River and a plague of locusts in the summer, followed by strong winds in the fall. The Chang River overflowed its banks in 1916, 1917, and 1918. This was followed in 1920 by a serious drought in which no significant rainfall was reported for a year. In 1921 a May hailstorm hurt spring crops and a sharp frost in March 1923 killed the spring wheat. There followed a number of years with annual flooding, causing much loss of life, property, and crops.[55] Hopei's Hsin-ho hsien recorded similar major disasters almost every year between 1913 and 1928.[56]

Altogether, Ta-ming hsien experienced seventeen major calamities during a twenty-one year period, and Hsin-ho hsien had fourteen major disasters during a sixteen-year period. Countless houses collapsed in the floods and sometimes entire *hsien* or villages were inundated. In years of drought there were no harvests in the fall and no opportunity to plant new seeds; the locusts left nothing at their departure. Youths and the middle-aged were forced to leave their villages to look for work in the cities or in some other area. Children and the old remained, unable to work the land and lacking even the essentials of life. Eventually those who remained were forced to sell their farm implements and houses. The poorest of all, having nothing to trade, were forced to sell their children.[57] The situation was sad indeed.

There were similar occurrences in other parts of China. In 1919, heavy rains near Nankung caused the river to overflow its banks and sweep over hundreds of miles of land.[58] In 1925, serious natural calamities occurred in Szechuan, Kueichou, Yunnan, Hunan, and Kiangsi. In Szechuan, 300,000 people starved.[59] Serious famine in Shensi and Kansu, in 1928 and 1929, caused 235,100 people to starve in a five-month period.[60] The worst calamity befell northern Szechuan in 1936 when a long drought hit the province. As food became scarce, people ate tree leaves; when the leaves were gone, some tried to eat a kind of clay called *kuan-yin*,[61] and others turned to cannibalism.[62] In northern Szechuan the meat of human beings was sold, and for many miles around the city of Sung-pang the ditches were filled with corpses of those who had starved to death.[63] One could see people trying to salvage these corpses for food, and some even ate their own sons and daughters.[64] Even grandchildren were not spared this fate, and it was reported that some people were cooked alive.[65] Other provinces may have suffered even more than Szechuan, which was traditionally called a Paradise Kingdom.

The third reason for the hard lives of the people was the excessively heavy taxes. From the beginning of the Republic, the warfare which engulfed China was carried out literally at the expense of the people in the provinces occupied by the warlords.[66] For example, an investigation of taxes paid by the people of Shantung in 1927 shows that the total amount collected was more than four times greater than taxes in the United States at the same time, and more than fourteen times greater than those paid in India.[67] An investigation into the land taxes paid in twelve provinces between 1920 and 1928 shows that they were collected continuously, some as many as thirty-one years in advance. In the case of Szechuan's Tzu-t'ung hsien, land taxes collected in the spring of 1926 were supposedly for the year 1957.[68] In 1933 taxes in Ch'eng-tu hsien of Szechuan were collected for the year 1979.[69] Other even more blatant cases were recorded.[70]

In April 1928 the Financial Affairs Department of the Chihli provincial government announced a special increase in taxes to meet military needs. After describing the new special taxes, officials admonished the citizens, saying, " . . . You should understand that these are basically taxes which the people ought to pay and they represent a form of assistance which the people should give."[71] This practice of constantly increasing land taxes became so excessive that people began to say it was better not to own land. Many people sold their land and others, sometimes to avoid the onerous taxes, fled to other areas.[72] In their view, local officials were not providing protection against natural disasters, but were always collecting money.[73] Naturally the most influential inhabitants tried various schemes to avoid payment, and when they were successful the burden was transferred to others.[74] Tax accounting by local governments became totally confused, and new taxes were instituted often, even when extremely large amounts were already being collected. Because some of Szechuan's *hsien* had as many as thirty-nine, fifty, or seventy-three times more money collected than was officially reported by government agencies,[75] the people of Szechuan bore a special burden.[76]

Excessive land taxes hurt the landowners, of course, but in the case of many special taxes no distinction was made between peasants and merchants. The merchants were often hit hardest. One example is the case of the Commercial Press of Ch'eng-tu in 1926, which, in transporting its goods, had to pay special taxes collected at no fewer than forty-four stations along the way. In travelling a distance of 395 *li*, its goods were taxed an average of every 10 *li*.[77] Goods of all types were heavily taxed at checkpoints set up along commercial roads. In one case, a load of rhubarb, weighing 134 *chin* and being transported a distance of about 1,000 *li* in Szechuan, paid 1,900 *yüan* in special taxes *in addition* to the normal taxes.[78]

The effects of numerous special taxes on transported goods were equally serious in Kuangtung province, where special taxes, usually for military purposes, were collected at many points, and even empty boats returning to their points of origin on the inland rivers had to pay heavy taxes.[79] Taxes also increased whenever warlord battles occurred. In 1926 in Kiangsi province, as a result of warlord fighting, sixteen new taxes were placed on merchant houses.[80]

For these reasons, the people, whose lives were already extremely bitter, were confronted with rising prices on all goods and a drop in the value of their money.[81] The lives led by ordinary people became harder and harder. As the quality of life deteriorated and banditry increased, the people were forced to band together in self-defense. Many local self-defense groups besides the Red Spears sprang up all over the country.[82]

Section 4: Social Background

By the beginning of the Republican period there were bandits almost everywhere in China.[83] There were many reasons for this, among them political factionalism, civil wars, natural disasters, and the bankruptcy of the peasant economy. Sometimes defeated warlord armies turned to banditry, plundering villages and taking whatever they desired. Several small bandit groups united to form gangs. The head of a gang was called the "master" or "shopkeeper."[84] Some of these gangs were very well organized.[85]

The warlords tried to strengthen themselves by recruiting bandit gangs. They gave military titles to bandit chieftains, the importance of the rank reflecting the size of the gang. This practice was expressed in a popular saying, "He who wants to be an official has only to muster a large group of bandits."[86] The Manchurian warlord, Chang Tso-lin, began as such a bandit chieftain. Hence, the country was full of bandits and without peace.

One of the more famous bandit leaders in 1921 was a chieftain known as Old Foreigner [Lao-yang-jen].[87] With a force of some thirty thousand men he attacked and occupied three cities. In September 1921, Old Foreigner and his gang looted and set fire to nine towns on the way to attack Cheng-yang. That night in the thirty miles between Hsi-hsien and Cheng-yang the fires burned until dawn.[88] The bandits massacred, raped, and burned after they captured the city of Cheng-yang. In September 1922 they moved into T'ai-ho hsien, taking many cities and burning entire villages to the ground.[89] Although they finally were subdued by the military governor, Chin Yün-p'eng,[90] we know the group remained alive, because in 1923 the warlord Wu P'ei-fu offered a military rank to its leader, Old Foreigner.[91] In similar ways other groups helped perpetuate the chaos that became endemic to China.

Another group, active in Yen-lin hsien, took a small town in May 1926 and murdered about one thousand inhabitants. In August they killed another fifteen hundred people and captured innumerable domestic animals in the north of the *hsien*.[92] Regardless of their size, when these bandit groups invaded a city almost nothing escaped destruction. They always killed many people, including women and children.[93] Other bandit groups specialized in kidnapping. The victims would be released after their families paid a ransom. The bandits sometimes referred to their victims as their "meal tickets" or as "Gods of Good Fortune," because the income from kidnapping was substantial.[94] In most cases families reported kidnappings to local authorities, but the officials considered such incidents commonplace and would take no action.[95]

Many other colorful terms were used by bandits to describe their kidnapped victims. Usually they were referred to as the "ticket." Foreign victims were called "foreign tickets," Chinese victims were called "basic tickets," and local victims were called "local tickets." Rich victims were called "lottery tickets" and the poor were called "pawn tickets."[98] As a group, victims were known as "meal tickets" (or "meat tickets"). The amount of money demanded as ransom depended on the wealth of the victim's family. Besides asking for money, which they called the "living dragon," bandits might demand horses, bullets, or opium.

One of the most striking aspects of bandit activity was the private courts they established to investigate the background of the victim's family and determine the proper ransom. The leader would himself act as chief judge. If the bandits felt their victims were deceiving them, or if they were dissatisfied with the ransom eventually paid, they would treat their victims cruelly.

The bandits had a wide range of cruel punishments, each given a colorful name. Some of them were:

1. *Eliminating Misfortune.* The victim was beaten if the kidnappers were chased by officials in the course of the kidnapping.
2. *Wearing Glasses.* The victim's eyes were covered with a cloth on which sticky medicine had been smeared.
3. *Smoking Eyes.* Smoke from burning rags or wood was blown into the victim's eyes.
4. *Lying in Mud.* The victim was made to lie naked in a trench which had been filled with mud.
5. *Sitting on the Toilet Pit.* This punishment was similar to the above, but feces were substituted for mud.
6. *Standing in Water.* The victim was made to stand naked in a pool or river with water up to the neck.
7. *The Leather Belt.* The victim was beaten with a leather belt.
8. *Burning the God of Good Fortune.* The victim's body was burned with lighted incense sticks.

9. *Taking a Cold Bath.* The victim's clothes were removed and cold water poured over him.
10. *On the Cross.* The victim was hung by his thumbs and his body swung back and forth by the bandits.
11. *Selling Bean Curd.* The victim's back was beaten with a belt until it swelled, then the swollen portion was cut in the size of pieces of bean curd and set on fire.
12. *Wrapping Felt.* The victim was wrapped in felt and the felt set on fire.
13. *Cutting the Ears.* The victim's ears were severed and sent to his family.
14. *Cutting the Fingers.* Same as above.
15. *Burning the Nipple.* The breasts were burned with a red-hot iron bar.
16. *Roasting the Back.* The victim's back was roasted over a stove.
17. *Tickling the Tendon.* Some of the victim's tendons were cut with a knife.
18. *Playing Cards.* If a female victim was not to be raped, the bandits removed her clothes and laid her on the floor, then played cards on her abdomen. They beat her whenever a card fell off.
19. *Drinking Hot and Sour Water.* Spicy or sour water, or gasoline, was poured down the victim's nose.
20. *Squeezing the Temples.* The temples were squeezed with a pair of chopsticks, causing blindness in the victim.[97]

These twenty punishments were fairly common among bandit groups, but variations or different punishments were practiced in other parts of the country. Listed below are some of the punishments practiced by bandits in Szechuan.

1. *Wearing Glasses.* Medicine was smeared on the victim's eyes, then he was forced to run blind.
2. *The Carpet Bed.* Thorns were placed on a bed and the victim was ordered to sleep naked on it.
3. *Carriage of Fire.* The victim was ordered to carry on his back a hot tank of burning charcoal.
4. *The Swimming Duck.* The victim's fingers and toes were tied with ropes. These were pulled in different directions as the victim lay face downward with heavy weights on his back.
5. *Long Nails.* Sharpened bamboo needles were stuck under the victim's nails.

6. *Housekeeping.* If the bandits had to leave the camp temporarily, they might nail the victim's feet to the floor.
7. *Hanging the Breast.* Women might have their nipples tied with strings which were hung from the ceiling and pulled taut.
8. *Swallowing Needles.* The victim was forced to swallow small needles.[98]

These punishments were most cruelly applied to wealthy victims to ensure that the ransom would be paid. In most cases the poor were simply released or killed. "Imprisoned" victims were usually tied up and their eyes covered with medicine so they could not see.[99] Sometimes as many as one hundred victims were imprisoned in one room, where they were forced to drink their own urine and many died of starvation.[100] If their families did not pay the ransom, they were tortured and finally killed. This was known as "tearing up the ticket."[101] In some cases, when families did not ransom their relatives, the "ticket bandits" struck again. For example, Honan's T'ai-k'ang hsien was struck four times in five years by kidnappers.[102] Bandits were everywhere, but information about them is often difficult to obtain.[103]

The government armies were supposed to control the bandits, but in fact the army leaders or warlords were only interested in expanding their power. Sometimes they obtained warrants to search houses for bandits, but actually this was a pretext for looting. If the householders resisted, they were arrested and accused of conniving with bandits. Many innocent people died this way. Warlords avoided fights with the bandits because the gangs were more often their friends than their enemies. Sometimes the bandits had better weapons than the government troops.[104] If a bandit chief commanded fifteen hundred men, he would be awarded a military rank by a warlord and incorporated into his army. In this way the warlord increased the number of men he commanded and their weapons.[105]

Thus, the warlords preferred increasing their armies to destroying the bandits. Many of their troops had been bandits originally. The armies and gangs would exchange information and cities were actually robbed by both sides.[106] A popular saying reflected the effectiveness of the troops in "suppressing" bandits: "The people cry while the bandits laugh."[107]

According to the evidence, there were at least fifty thousand bandits in Hunan province in 1925. Many of their leaders were well known. We can only guess how many more operated there whose names and numbers have not been recorded. Possibly there were more than one hundred thousand bandits in the 111 *hsien* of Hunan province. If this is true, there were an average of about one thousand bandits in each *hsien*, though some *hsien* such as Ling-ju hsien recorded as many as twelve thousand. Because they were so numerous, a popular folksong in Hunan ran, "During the day we dare not go outside; at night we fear the barking dogs. If we hear the sound of a rifle, we are frightened out of our wits."[108]

A common problem in most areas was that funds were limited and local police could not defend the people. Some localities, like Hsin-yang hsien, tried various plans between 1914 and 1925, with police forces of between 53 and 250 persons, but they faced the constant problem of obtaining sufficient funds to pay the men. The cost of maintaining police forces continued to rise and usually the money had to come from local sources such as the wealthy gentry in the area.[109] Often their weapons were inadequate, and this too greatly reduced the effectiveness of local police against the bandits.[110] In some localities the police not only could not erradicate bandits, but they could not protect the people or local government offices.[111] The bandits only grew stronger, and some groups even used cannons.[112] Under these dangerous and unstable conditions, more and more people turned to the Red Spears' philosophy, with its supposed protection from harm gained by swallowing amulets. They began to form Red Spears societies.[113] These and other secret societies sprang up throughout the countryside.[114]

Section 5: Religious Background

Before 1940 the peasants of China believed in numerous deities. Almost every rock, river, or blade of grass had its own god, as did the gate of the house and the family hearth; even oxen and horses were protected by spirits. Religious beliefs extended to devils, ghosts, and shamans who could ward off sickness or evil.[115] Such popular beliefs became a part of China's history and the names of deities were often recorded in official annals.[116] That various forms of magic and intervention by the gods were often connected with the birth of the founder of a dynasty is evident in official histories from the earliest times through the Ch'ing dynasty. Early rulers used stories of this sort to assert their immortality, claiming to be the sons of gods, and therefore divine. This made dynastic changes seem ordained by the gods as well, and each new ruler tried to establish his legitimacy by claiming to have their blessing. Regardless of the manner in which a new ruler ascended the throne, the people were told to worship him unquestioningly, and any opposition was punishable by death.

Such strongly held beliefs were not easily overcome. Even the government of the early Republic, which tried to stop these superstitious practices, was unable to do so. In the words of a popular song, "First worship the Buddha, then worship the gods, then you will have peace the entire year."[117]

When faced with grave difficulties, as peasants usually were in the Republican period, they could only turn to their gods for assistance. They could not protect themselves from the disasters caused by soldiers and bandits, so they joined societies like the Red Spears, which claimed to offer divine protection by harnessing the power of the gods.

Chapter III: Organization and Beliefs

Section 1: Organization

The Red Spears evolved from the Boxers, and its organization was basically inherited from the village militia. It was a rural organization based in the villages and small towns. Usually each village had an assembly hall [*hui-t'ang*], although occasionally a number of villages would jointly sponsor one assembly hall. The society members would invite an old Taoist priest to lead them in ritual chanting and worship of the spirits. After members had learned the magic arts, the priest would leave and one of the regular members would assume his duties. The man in charge of ceremonies was called the grand master [*ta-shih-hsiung*] and the members addressed each other as brother. The business affairs of the society were handled by the village headman or by a member of the local gentry, and items such as tea, kerosene, and incense were provided by the wealthier families in the vicinity.

In times of danger, society members, would obey the instructions of the grand master. Where there were many members other leaders would be appointed. These were called the second grand master, third grand master, and so on. They were expected to assist the grand master in his ceremonial duties and to carry out his instructions. The grand master was said to be following the instructions of the spirits. Spirits were the highest authority within the society.

Sometimes each Red Spears unit was called a school [*hsüeh*] and the leader called the schoolmaster [*hsüeh-chang*]. In other places the local leaders might be called company commanders [*lien-chang*] or regimental commanders [*tui-chang*]. The units under these leaders were known as ranks [*p'ai*] or squads [*pan*]. Above the local leaders were the camp commanders [*ying-chang*] and the unit commanders [*t'uan-chang*]. Unit commanders tended to be the most powerful, and a unit usually comprised several local branches or "schools."[1]

31

Unit commanders were supposed to be individuals of some influence, so the leadership of the Red Spears often consisted of rich peasants, landlords, or gentry.[2] The units and society branches in various locations considered themselves equal and did not rank themselves hierarchically. Normally there was little regular contact between branches of the society, but in times of emergency branches in several hundred villages or several *hsien* could quickly unite in a single formidable force.[3]

Although spirits were the highest authorities within the society, the will of the spirits was expressed by the grand master, so in fact he held the real authority and even had the power of life and death. When an important situation arose, incense was lit and the spirits were asked for instructions. These instructions were reported to the society by the grand master. When the spirits were asked for advice, the grand master would sit silently next to the altar. A single word such as "yes," "no," "live," or "die," assumed to be the instructions he had received, would decide the matter. Unit commanders and other commanders did not have this authority. Later some officers were appointed above the unit-commander rank, and called brigade commanders [*lu-chang*], general commanders [*tsung-chih-hui*], and commanders-in-chief [*tsung-szu-ling*]. Some of the authority reserved for the grand master later fell into the hands of these high officers.

In 1923 Wu P'ei-fu was defeated at the Shan-hai pass. He attempted to use the strength of the Red Spears by appointing thousands of their leaders, such as Yin Tzu-hin, Lou Pai-hsün, and Kao Hsien-chou, brigade commanders in the Honan army.[4] Because there were so many branches and factions in the Red Spears, and despite the influence of the society throughout the country, there were many differences in names, titles, and organizations within the parent groups. For example, a person who held the title commander of the society [*tsung-hui-chang*], was later called the *tu-pan*, and in Honan's Yung-yang hsien the headquarters of the Red Spears was known as the office of the *tu—pan* [*tu-pan kung-shu*] in imitation of the titles of regular government officies. On occasion it was called the general headquarters [*szu-ling-pu*], and the society's leader, Chang Ching-wang, was known either as *tu-pan* or commander-in-chief [*tsung-szu-ling*]. The officers under him were the general master [*tsung-chiao-shih*] (in Yung-yang hsien a man named Li Ch'ing-lung), the chief-of-staff [*t'san-mo-chang*] (a man named Shih Hua-nan), and the sworn brothers [*chieh-pai hsiung-ti*] (four men named Kuo Hung-pin, Li Chia-yen, Wang Chih-kang, and Chin Feng-yao).[5]

Based as it was on military or government models, the organization of the society eventually grew quite complex. It was divided into a civil section [*wen-t'uan-pu*] and a military section [*wu-t'uan-pu*]. The civil section concerned itself with records, finance, and litigation. The military section directed drill, weapons training, and the use of magic charms.[6] Local organizations might expand to include several score or even several hundred villages, so that a single *hsien* might be divided into eastern, western, southern, and northern sectors. Each sector was headed by a unit leader [*t'uan-tsung*]. Leaders of this rank might also be called the leader [*ts'ung-t'ou*], the society leader [*tsung-hui-chang*], or the sector head [*fang-tsung*]. These leaders were responsible for administration in their sectors. The sectors were occasionally called wards [*ch'ü*], in which case the leader was a ward head [*ch'ü-chang*]. Thus, a single organization could encompass several wards or an entire *hsien*.

In 1927, the leader of the Red Spears in southern Honan, Chang Meng-hu, commanded over 100,000 men. The troops he controlled were divided into three wards. The first as commanded by Chang Ting-shan and consisted of over 40,000 members. It covered Nan-yang hsien and Hsin-yeh hsien. The second ward was commanded by Liu Hu-tzu and contained over 35,000 members. It covered Hsin-yang hsien and Lo-shan hisen. The third ward, headed by Hou Tzu-ching, had over 20,000 members and included Szu-p'ing hsien and Wu-yang hsien. Some of the other Red Spears leaders in Honan were Liu San, who commanded about 53,000 members in Sha-ho hsien and Yeh-ch'eng; Wang K'un-ju, who commanded about 80,000 members in Yung-yang hsien and Kung hsien; Li San-ma-tzu, who commanded about 110,000 members in K'ai-feng and Cheng-chou; and Yang Kuo-hsin and Ma Fei-t'ien, who led about 120,000 members in Hsiu-wu hsien, Chih-hsien, and An-yang hsien.[7] In Hopei province, the Red Spears leader, Chao Ch'eng-ch'iu, commanded about 40,000 members in Tz'u-hsien and Yung-nien hsien. I Sheng-lei commanded about 30,000 members in Kuang-p'ing hsien and Ta-ming hsien. Ts'ai Yung-fa commanded about 25,000 members in Hei-lung kuan and Hsi-huang ts'un. Wang Lao-wu commanded over 10,000 members in Tung-ming hsien and Ch'ang-yüan hsien. In Shantung province, Leader Lu Kuei commanded over 10,000 members in Chia-hsiang hsien and Chi-ning hsien. Chou Fu-sheng commanded some 30,000 members in Kao-t'ang hsien and Ch'ing-p'ing hsien.[8] Based on these figures and evidence from other sources, we can speculate that in Honan province alone there were at least 1.5 million Red Spears members. If we add the membership in Chihli, Anhwei, and Shantung provinces, the total will be more than 3 million.[9]

Although these proven figures seem high, the actual totals were even greater. According to Chang Yung-te, an official sent by the Republican government to lead the Red Spears in southern Hopei, "The area from the northern bank of the Yellow River to Kung-hsien encompasses over thirty *hsien*, and almost all the males between the ages of fifteen and sixty are members of the Red Spears; this implies a total membership of not less that two million individuals."[10] At that time the weapons of the Red Spears consisted of traditional spears, rifles, and handguns. Their strength was sufficient not only to control banditry, but to challenge government forces as well. In 1937, after the Marco Polo Bridge Incident, the Red Spears again became noticeably active in north China. During the War of Resistance Against Japan, their organization and the titles of their leaders changed again. Besides the leader [*hui-chang*] and the master [*fa-shih*] (also called at times the grand master), the chiefs were known by such titles as battalion commander [*ta-tui-chang*], company commander [*hsiao-tui-chang*], detachment commander [*chih-tui-chang*], and so on.

Section 2: Discipline

Since they organized to protect families and homes, the Red Spears naturally drew their strength from the people. Initially they were led by local gentry or clan elders, who, because of their traditional positions of strength and authority in the community, were able to preserve the best of traditional village customs. They also acted locally to preserve law and order. Thus, when they were first organized, the Red Spears acted responsibly and were highly disciplined. After their numbers grew and diverse elements joined the society, the members could not be counted on to act in a responsible and positive way. Because of this there was a pledge, taken upon entrance into the society, which reads, "Do not dare to pick a flower or break a twig [i.e., seduce or rape women], for if you do so you will be shot; do not dare to do an evil deed just for the sake of wickedness, for if you do so you will be shot through the head."[11]

There were four general rules for Red Spears members.

1. Do not rape women.
2. Do not loot and steal.

3. Do not commit murder or arson.
4. Do not profane spirits and gods.[12]

There were various degrees of punishment for those who disobeyed the regulations. The lightest punishment was a severe beating; the most serious punishment was death.[13] Society members were strictly prohibited from raping women or profaning spirits and gods, because it was felt these acts would cause the spirits to abandon the membership, rendering their magical ceremonies useless and destroying their immunity to bullets.

After 1921, the number of Red Spears members increased greatly, but along with the growth came many unsavory elements such as vagabonds and bandits. Because of this the traditional leaders, local gentry and clan elders, could no longer maintain control over the society. At this time the society began to be used by local tyrants and evil gentry. After the leadership of the Red Spears was transferred to such people, the character of many branches changed, and crimes such as looting and killing by society members became so numerous that often there was no difference between Red Spears units and the common bandits. In the end no uniform rules were followed by society members.

Some government officials and politicians wished to tap the strength of the Red Spears, so they devised a number of regulations that were supposed to apply to the society. Typical examples are as follows:

1. This society is an armed organization, which has as its goal the establishment of self-defense, self-government, and peace for the people.
2. Members of this society will abide by the following maxims:

    A. Respect your parents and seniors.
    B. Love your home and your country.
    C. Always be honest.
    D. Face difficulties together.
    E. Protect public property and the law.
    F. Do not recklessly commit crimes.

3. This society, in order to promote self-government and self-defense, will undertake the following responsibilities:

A. Destroy bandits.
B. Eliminate outlaw armies.
C. Refuse to pay illegal taxes or recognize
   tax increases, and oppose corvée labor.
D. Oppose corrupt officials, bandits,
   and troublemakers.

4. All citizens of the Republic of China who are at least eighteen
   years of age and in possession of some property are eligible to
   join this society if they are recommended by two members, if
   they take the society oath, and if they pay the membership fee
   of one *yüan*.
   The oath for entrance into the society was as follows:

   I _____, a resident of _____ province,
   _____ *hsien*, and _____ village, having
   been recommended by _____ and
   _____, wish to join the society. I swear to
   obey the regulations of the society. If I disobey
   them I will accept the punishment given to me.

   Seal of the new member

   Seal of the first person
   recommending new member

   Seal of second person
   recommending new member

   Document of the Red Spears

   Date

5. The military organization of this society is as follows:

   Every 5 members comprise a *wu*, which has a
   commanding officer.

   Every 5 *wu* (25 members) comprise a *tui*, which
   has a commanding officer.

Every 5 *tui* (125 members) comprise a *she*, which has a commanding officer.

Every 5 *she* (625 members) comprise a *hsiang*, which has a commanding officer.

Every 5 *hsiang* (3,125 members) comprise a *t'ing*, which has a commanding officer.

Every 5 *t'ing* (15,625 members) comprise a *chün*, which has a commanding officer.

Every 5 *chün* (78,125 members) comprise a *lu*, which has a commanding officer.

Every 5 *lu* (390,625 members) comprise a *chen*, which has a commanding officer.

Every 5 *chen* (1,953,125 members) comprise a *tou*, which has a commanding officer.

Every 5 *tou* (9,766,625 members) comprise a *fang*, which has a commanding officer.

Every 5 *fang* (48,828,125 members) comprise a *t'ung*, which has a commanding officer.

The *t'ung* commander will be appointed from among the five *fang* commanders. This practice will be followed throughout the hierarchy of units, so that, for example, the *tou* commander will be appointed from among the five *chen* commanders, and so on. At the lowest level, the five members of each *wu* will elect their own leader.

6. Members of the society will obey their superiors.
7. All rewards and punishments will be carried out according to military law.
8. Besides the burning of incense, the reciting of magic formulae, and so on, all members will be instructed in military and political ideology.
9. All members of the society, when on duty, will be considered mobilized for the protection of local areas. When not on duty, they should act as ordinary people, work hard, and not allow themselves to be used by bad people.

10. Society members should always ensure that their actions contribute to the goal of promoting local self-government, regardless of whether they are following old regulations or implementing the rules of new organizations.

11. It is acceptable for members to bring into the society friends who are members of other groups such as the Yellow Spears, Green Spears, Colorful Spears, the Descendants [Sun-chih], the Great Spirit, and other societies that have the same goals of self-defense and self-government.

12. It is acceptable to assist friends from other groups who wish to unite with our society to form cooperative organizations.

13. In times of emergency, society members should gather in their assigned locations and obey the instructions of their commanders.

14. In times of unexpected attack from outside forces, all must unite with members of the society nationwide and, remembering the policy of protecting the nation, form a united front against the enemy.

15. The expenses of the society will be borne by individual members based on their ability to contribute. In cases where special assistance is needed, those who contribute more than ten *yüan* on one occasion will be chosen as chief committee member [*chu-jen wei-yüan*].

16. Nonmembers of the Red Spears who contribute more than ten *yüan* on one occasion will be named honorable contributors.

17. Members who violate the regulations will be tried.

18. Sentences resulting from a trial will be based on standard military regulations or the normal criminal statutes.

19. All members of other societies who follow these regulations will be considered members of our society and we will assist them.

20. These regulations will take effect as soon as they are promulgated and, if unacceptable, can be revised at meetings of the society.[14]

There are some strange aspects to these regulations. For example, regulation 4 states that individuals "in possession of some property" and able to "pay the membership fee of one *yüan*" are eligible to join the society. In fact, in the records of most members of the society, there is no reference to property ownership or payment of a fee. Regulation 5, concerning the organization of the society, is also suspect. Although the Red Spears leaders were capable persons, how could anyone control 9,766,625 people, as a *fang* commander was supposed to do? The 48,828,125 men supposedly under the control of a *t'ung* commander is an equally exaggerated figure. Regulation 7, referring to the application of military law in the case of rewards and punishments, is unrealistic as well. We must ask ourselves how many members of the Red Spears, civilians in particular, would be familiar with military law? Regulation 15 states that those contributing more than ten *yüan* would be named the chief committee member, but there was no such title in the Red Spears organization. Also, the practice mentioned in regulation 16, that of naming nonmembers who contribute more than ten *yüan* "honorable contributors," does not coincide with actual society procedures. In sum, the regulations appear to have been a fabrication, an attempt to use the Red Spears for a particular purpose. It is doubtful that these regulations were ever implemented by the Red Spears leadership or followed by its members.

Section 3: Aims and Purposes

After the establishment of the Republic, in order to protect themselves and their property and to provide for mutual assistance, the people organized such groups as the Red Spears, the Heavenly Gate Society, the Yellow Shirt Society, the White Tassel Society, the Green Tassel Society, as so on.[15]

Originally these societies were formed to guard against banditry but, when the regular armies proved unable to control the bandits and law and order deteriorated, the people transferred their hatred from the bandits to the soldiers. Trouble often developed between the Red Spears and government troops, sometimes resulting in armed attacks.[16] As a result the Red Spears had to fight both bandits and troops that acted like bandits.[17] In a typical situation, when villagers discovered a bandit gang or marauding military force, an alarm would be sounded by ringing a bell, beating a drum, or firing a cannon. Society members from surrounding villages would gather with their spears and cannon. Believing themselves safe from death, they would attack bravely and fight until a victory was won.[18] In response to the strength of the Red Spears, bandits dispersed, soldiers could not advance, and law and order was maintained. Their effectiveness was clearly demonstrated and their goals attained.

Their basic purposes were stated in regulation 3: to destroy bandits; eliminate outlaw armies; refuse to pay illegal taxes or honor tax increases; and oppose corrupt officials, bandits, and troublemakers.[19]

After the Japanese invasion of Manchuria in 1931, the Red Spears and Big Sword units in the northeast adopted slogans such as "Protect the Nation, the People, and Our Homes," "Crush Japanese Imperialism," and "Overthrow Manchoukuo" [the Japanese puppet state set up in the northeast in 1932].

Soon after the Marco Polo Bridge Incident in 1937, when all of north China was taken over by the Japanese, the Red Spears society became active again. Although its avowed purpose was still to guard against bandits, its real aim was to oppose Japanese forces in the area. In March 1938, for example, Japanese troops were attacked by Red Spears units on the T'ang-yin-hsun Highway. Several hundred Japanese were killed or wounded, and many weapons captured. Records exist of similar attacks on Japanese troops in north China during 1939 and 1943. The Japanese often suffered heavy losses, prompting them, on at least one occasion, to return later and massacre villagers.

The Japanese troops were Buddhists and believed in rebirth. Very often Red Spears members, besides their tasseled spears, carried broadswords which they used to decapitate the enemy during the course of a battle. Japanese scalps were treated as symbols of victory. Although the Japanese *bushido* code held that soldiers should not fear death, they did fear decapitation. According to their beliefs, a headless person could not be reborn and his spirit would wander endlessly, without rest. As a result, the Japanese troops greatly feared the Red Spears. After 1942 there were large areas beyond the towns, cities, and transport lines in Shantung, Hopei, and Honan which Japanese troops refused to enter due to their fear of decapitation.

Chapter IV: Ceremonies and Ritual Practices

Section 1: Ceremonies of Initiation

Initiation ceremonies were an important part of Red Spears ritual. Initiations were always held in rooms or temples that could accommodate several score people. After an altar was erected the room was usually referred to as the inner chamber [nei-ch'ang], although it also might be known as the meeting hall [hui-t'ang], study hall [hsüeh-t'ang], ceremonial hall [li-t'ang], Buddha hall [fu-t'ang], holy hall [fa-t'ang], or palace of peace [an-kung].[1]

The altar, called the spirit platform [shen-t'ai] was usually a narrow table, four or five feet in height. It was placed against one wall. On the wall above the altar a spirit scroll was hung, on which was written the name of the deity to be worshipped. The scroll was usually made of yellow paper, although red paper or even a wooden tablet might be used. The spirit worshipped by each branch of the society varied according to time and place. On either side of the spirit scroll or table were hung matching couplets [tui-lien].[2] These might contain phrases such as "The Spirit Worshipped by the People Descends to the Altar to Instruct; The Brothers and Sons Burn Incense and Recite Prayers," or "Sitting in Silence Meditating on the Enlightened One; Listening and Talking about How Mere Humans Are Not True Spirits." A horizontal banner hung above the altar contained phrases such as "Buddhist Teaching Everywhere" [fu-fa wu-pien]. An incense pot was placed in the center of the altar, with two candles on either side. Other items such as emblems, incense, and paper were placed on the altar as well. A lower table was positioned before the altar and held various foods.

When a ceremony was to be held, the master would be asked to lead it. Then the initiate and the two persons who had recommended him, after receiving approval from the master, would begin. Initiation into the society was termed "entering school" [shang-hsüeh]. Before "entering school," initiates had to abstain from eating three types of prohibited food: wild geese, quail, and pigeon (the three prohibited heavenly foods); dog, horse, and cow (the three prohibited earthly foods); prawns, turtle, and loach fish (the three prohibited seafoods). This prohibition was to remain in effect forever.[3]

On the day of "entering school," initiates had to bathe thoroughly and abstain from sexual intercourse. In fact, they were not to have had sexual intercourse within the previous hundred days. In order to sincerely honor the master, their "teacher," initiates would perform ritual prostrations, kneeling three times and touching their heads to the floor nine times. After this procedure they would perform a ritual kowtow: gathering before the altar, shoulders bared, making two fists which they placed on the ground, then kneeling and touching their heads to their fists. Candles and incense were burning on the altar. To the right was a large turtle candle (usually a kerosene lantern which somewhat resembled a turtle, but occasionally a shallow bowl filled with clear oil in which a wick was placed). To the left was a large bowl filled with cold water. After reciting a magic formula, each initiate would draw a magic charm with a brush. The charm was burned and its ashes mixed with water from the bowl. Then each initiate would sip the mixture. Afterwards the initiates would turn to receive secret instructions from the master, though not before vowing to the spirits never to divulge these orders. If they did so they were to be rent by lightening. The vows were as follows.

> Your majesty's disciple _____, who today will enter upon the Great Way, who will be transformed, and will safeguard the regulations of this society,
>
> 1. Will not dare to commit crimes. If I do so I will be shot in the head.
> 2. Will not dare to pick a flower or break a willow [seduce or rape women]. If I do so I will be shot in the heart.
> 3. Will honor my parents.
> 4. Will respect my teacher and leaders.
> 5. Will join others in doing what needs to be done.
> 6. Will work hard every day and exert my total energy in accomplishing the tasks at hand.[4]

After taking these vows, the master would teach the initiates the method for praying to the spirits. Then he would take sticks of incense from the censor and, breaking them in two, give half a stick to each initiate. The master then would replace his incense sticks and bow to the Buddha. Next he would inhale and, exhaling audibly, stamp the ground with his right foot. The initiates would imitate the actions of the master. The master then would take an incense stick and move toward the entrance, stopping just inside, then bowing and proceeding through the door. Outside he would call on the spirits to assemble. To call the spirits he first would face north, bow his head, raise his incense, and recite, "Your Majesty's disciple requests the Jade Emperor [Yü-huang lao-yeh] to leave his heavenly palace and approach to receive our offering [wen-hsiang, lit. 'to smell the incense']. I also request the Golden Boy and Jade Girl [Chin-t'ung yü-nü] to leave their heavenly palace and receive our offering." After reciting these phrases, the master would raise his incense stick in honor of the spirits, then kneel and touch his head to the ground.

Turning toward the southeast, the master would repeat these actions, saying, "Your Majesty's disciple requests the Goddess of Mercy [Kuan-yin lao-mu] to leave her mountaintop palace and approach to receive our offering. I also request the Golden Boy and Jade Girl to leave their mountaintop palace and receive our offering." Finally, turning to the southwest, the master would say, "Your Majesty's disciple requests the Honorable Ancestor [Tzu-shih lao-yeh] to leave his golden mountaintop palace and receive our offering. I also ask that the spirits of the Duke of Chou [Chou kung-tzu], the Sages of T'ao-hua [T'ao-hua-hsien], the Flag-bearing General [Ch'ang-ch'i-chiang], the Guardian General [Chin-k'ang-chiang], the Black Tiger [Hei-hu], the Holy Officials [Ling-kuan], the Turtle and Snake Generals [Kuei-she-chiang], and all the ancestors leave their golden mountaintop and receive our offering."

After facing the three directions, the master would return the incense to the altar. Upon reentering the room he would say "Your Majesty's disciple asks the ancestors to enter the temple and receive our offering." When the incense was replaced in the censor, the portion of the ceremony known as "calling the spirits" was concluded.

The second part of the ceremony was called "dressing the body" [chuang shen-tzu], which referred to ritual purification or cleansing. Society members would kneel before the altar and the master would crumple above the censor a printed magic charm. While the charm was burning the master would take a deep breath and silently recite a magic formula while moving his right hand backward. He would then place his right hand near the candle flame and, taking a deep breath, suck the flame into his mouth. He would turn to face the members, with his right hand positioned beneath his mouth, and exhale on the body of each initiate, moving from the top of the head to the chest, then to the face, and back to the top of the head. These actions were repeated, the master now exhaling down the initiates's back, from the head to the waist, then up to the head again. A third exhalation would cleanse the arms from the palms to the shoulders, first on the left side, then on the right. It was said that with this ceremony the initiate's body was transformed from ordinary [*fan t'i*] to holy [*fa-t'i*]. Only after such a ceremony did the new members have bodies into which the spirits could descend [*chiang-shen fu-ti*].

Once "dressed," members had to learn self-protection. Before undertaking any mission, members would kneel, fold their hands to their chests, and recite the magic formula for protecting the body: "Heaven protect me, Earth protect me, the Front protect me, the Back protect me, Right protect me, Left protect me. Goddess of Mercy protect me in front, Goddess of Lishan [Li-shan lao-mu] protect me in the rear. Ancestors protect me, the Five Thunder Spirits [Wu-lei-k'ang] especially protect me." Then they would recite the charm for protection against bullets: "Oh Buddha [Wu-liang-fu], I have asked the Holy Emperor [Sheng-ti lao-yeh] to protect me. Five Thunder Spirits, I have asked the Ancestors to protect me against bullets. May the Green Dragon [Ch'ing-lung] sacrifice to the five Holy Spirits [Wu-kan-shen] that the bullets will fall around me. May they fall of their own accord. I took the clear spring waters, the burning ashes, into my stomach and have special clothing to protect me from bullets, all this zealously done according to your instructions."[5] Each time the incantation was recited, the hands would be raised to the forehead and the phrase repeated in one long breath. Chanting in this manner, with repeated prostrations, was called "sending off the spirits" [*sung-shen*]. With this the initiation ceremony came to a close.

Because the Red Spears had many branches, there was no standard initiation ceremony. Usually each ceremony had three stages, called the "three fields" [*san-ch'ang*]. The first stage was called the "level field" [*p'ing-ch'ang*] or "opening field" [*k'ai-fang-ch'ang*]. The second stage was the "running field" [*k'uai-pao-ch'ang*], and the third was called the "black tiger field" [*hei-hu-ch'ang*]. Occasionally the ceremonies had only one stage, so there was no standard method of organization.

Part of the preparation for any society ritual was abstention from certain foods. For example, members were prohibited from eating wild goose, because these birds mate with a single partner for life. Out of respect for this fidelity, goose was not eaten. Quail and pigeon are similar birds and these three comprised the three prohibited heavenly foods. Members also abstained from eating dogs, horses, and cattle. Dogs guard the gates of houses, while horses and cattle work in the fields. Who could enjoy eating animals which almost become friends? These prohibitions actually reflected the traditional values of any rural agricultural society. It is reasonable that dogs, horses, and cattle were known as the prohibited earthly foods. The prawn was thought to be good for the kidneys, the turtle good for the liver, and the loach fish helped calm the stomach.[6] They were called the three prohibited seafoods because the peasants believed that they were aids in cleansing the body and preserving youthful vigor and contained rich sexual hormones; young men would often cause trouble after eating such food.

The Red Spears worshipped a number of deities in the pantheon of popular gods. At least twenty-three such deities can be named. Among them are the Child-Giving Goddess of Mercy [Sung-tzu Kuan-yin]; the God of War, Kuan-ti [Kuan-sheng ti-chün]; the Twelve Lohan [Shih-erh lo-han]; and the canonized folk hero, Chu-ke Liang. Many of the deities were historical figures from popular romances such as the *Romance of the Three Kingdoms* [San-kuo yen-yi]. Practically, the only historical figures not worshipped were traitors or bandits such as Sung Chiang, a character in the *Water Margin* [Shui-hu chuan].

One very popular folk deity who was not worshipped was Ma-tzu [the Goddess of Fishermen, also called the Holy Mother], widely esteemed in southeast China. This reflects the fact that the Red Spears was a land-based organization, and the popular beliefs of fishermen and boat people did not take hold. Although the Red Spears spread as far as the coastal provinces of southeast China, its rituals and patron gods remained the traditional deities worshipped in the inland areas.

Section 2: Secret Teachings

The Red Spears was sometimes referred to as the Red Study Society [Hung-hsüeh-hui] because its rituals included a large number

of magical practices which constituted a sort of "secret learning."
The organization was divided into the Great Red Study group, also
known as the Old Buddha Hall [Lao-fu-ch'ang]; the Middle Red Study
group [Chung-hung-hsüeh]; and the Small Red Study group
[Hsiao-hung-hsüeh]. These can be said to correspond to the divisions
of university, middle school, and primary school. The middle and
small groups believed in such practices as eating amulets as a means
of protection against bullets.[7]

Although they differed in some specific practices, most of these
groups divided their meeting halls into an inner chamber and an
outer chamber. The outer chamber was for public meetings and
lectures and the inner chamber was for rituals. The inner chamber
was silent and still. Women, referred to as "black-headed yin^a
people," were forbidden to enter, to hear secret formula, to
participate in ceremonies, or to practice kung-fu. The secret
teachings were taught by the master who also led the assembled
members in ritual washing and rinsing of the mouth. To begin, the
master would enter the temple with incense and recite a magical
phrase. The assembled members would follow and kowtow before
the altar.

In the Red Spears society, ritual practices were coupled with
actual military training, and a schedule for both was usually
observed. For example, on the first day of the ceremonies, the members would kneel at the altar until one incense stick had burned about
four inches. Then they would practice kung-fu. On the second day
they would kneel until one-half of the stick burned before practicing
kung-fu. In this manner their abilities improved and the time spent
kneeling lengthened. The longer one could kneel, the greater was the
protection dispensed by the spirits. Those who could kneel for four
days were protected against knives and those who managed to kneel
a full forty-eight days were protected against guns. A person whose
body, standing erect, supposedly could deflect bullets and was as
strong as a wall of steel was said to have become a master.[8] Very
few completed this training and became masters; the typical society
member was somewhere in the middle of his training.

Practices of the Red Spears varied according to locality and the
particular branch of the society. Some of the most common
variations are outlined below.

1. *Seizing the Spirit.* For this ceremony, the society members
   would gather every evening in the meeting hall. After washing
   their hands and rinsing their mouths, incense would be burned.

The master would ask the assembled members to kneel before the altar and shut their eyes tightly. Magic formulae would be spoken. Next each member would reach into the air, as if grasping it, and put the palm of his hand over his mouth. Then he would inhale as noisily as possible. The process was repeated as many as thirty or forty times, and the meeting hall would be filled with the sounds of the men inhaling. If the still-burning incense stick had remained black when the "seizing of the spirits" [chao-kung] was completed, it was taken to mean that something would happen against which the members should guard.

"Seizing the spirit" required repeated deep breathing. After long periods of practice, many members really did improve their stamina through these deep-breathing exercises. The peasants thought the increased stamina was due to magic. When the incense stick was declared to have remained black after burning, the master no doubt had prior information about some impending event. Actually, after these incense sticks were burnt they were a reddish-black color, and could be described as either black or red. Naturally it would more effectively arouse the society members, with their belief in the great power of the spirits, if the color was taken as a sign from their deities. Members always accepted the decision of the master in matters of reading signs sent by the spirits.

2. *Eating the Ashes of an Amulet.* The Red Spears members placed great value on eating the ashes of a magic amulet, so much so that they believed that this practice would prevent injury by knives or bullets. Most of the amulets were yellow papers inscribed in cinnabar red. Cinnabar as used as a tonic in traditional Chinese medicine and was believed to calm the nerves and help persons in shock. It also could cause mental deficiency if too much was eaten.[9]

The yellow paper used for the amulet was a thin sort of tissue. Yellow was a color reserved for the spirits. The paper was composed of saltpeter and potassium nitrate (Kno_3) and had medicinal properties as a stimulant. Thus, after eating the paper's ashes, the society member might experience hallucinations in which perceived colors would change. Sometimes his eyes would roll and he would moan as if sick. Ordinary peasants believed symptoms were caused by a spirit which had descended into the human body and taken control.

This belief was shared by Red Spears members who wished to bolster their courage before a battle or attack. The leaders probably realized that this practice was a most effective way of strengthening the members' courage and resolve, so they used the ritual rather than denouncing it.

3. *Reciting Magic Formulae.* The practice of reciting magic formulae was important for two reasons. First, ordinary peasants commonly recited magic formulae whenever they were confronted with frightening or dangerous situations, thus calling upon the spirits to protect them. Second, members of the Red Spears would close their eyes and silently recite a magic formula in front of their altars at home after the evening meal. They would recite without moving their lips, causing saliva to accumulate in the mouth. Periodically this was swallowed with a loud gulp. They believed this saliva would help ensure a long and healthy life. (A noted specialist at the University of Tokyo, Professor Ogata Tomasaburō, lent credence to this theory with this announcement that saliva contains a hormone, patotin, which helps preserve youthful vigor.) Certainly saliva aids digestion, and is in general considered essential in a healthy body.

4. *Dressing the Body.* Once the society members were assembled and kneeling before the altar, the grand master would eat the ashes of an amulet, recite a magic formula, and clasp his hands together. Then, from the palms of his hands he would blow at the bodies of the members, moving from the head to the feet, all the while standing with his left leg extended forward slightly, his weight on his right leg. When finished he would blow three times, and this was called "dressing the body." It was said that once the body was ceremonially dressed in such a manner it was transformed from an ordinary body to a holy body, into which the spirits could descend and temporarily reside. Having completed this ceremonial dressing, the society member would kneel before the altar and recite magic formula, after which the spirit could descend into his body. It was considered proper to dress the body before undertaking any mission.

It can be said that the practice of feeling a spirit descending into the body was a form of hypnotism, and it should be clear that the Red Spears leaders effectively combined a scientific phenomenon with the superstitions of the common people. We cannot dismiss these practices out of hand because of their effectiveness and the importance of the society's goal.

5. *The Spirit Descending into the Body.* The descent of a spirit into the body was directed by the grand master, the second master, or by any devout believer who might call a spirit into his own body. Standing before the altar, the grand master would eat the ashes of an amulet and, with both eyes shut and hands clasped in prayer, recite a magic formula. After about twenty minutes his hands would begin to shake and his lips would move as if in speech. Once in this trance, he would sit upon a chair, his eyes still shut. It was said that the spirit had entered his body. If called upon to speak, the spirit would respond. If it was a literary spirit, it would answer in elegant and articulate language. If it was a military spirit, the possessed person might jump up wildly, grab a spear or gun, and dance about with great strength. After about an hour the possessed person would sink to the ground and slowly return to normal. This was called "leaving of holiness" [*t'ui-fa*].

Occasionally one would encounter a person unable to eject the spirit from his body, even after three or four hours. These people were described as having faces of a ghostly color and eyes of green.[10] They could be relieved of the spirit by the grand master or a Buddhist priest who would drink from a bowl of cold water, recite a magic formula, and spit the water at the face of the possessed person while rubbing a spot on his hand between the thumb and the index finger.[11]

Nonmembers were forbidden to witness this spirit possession, so very few people outside the society ever saw it. It was said that novices and nonbelievers were incapable of accepting a spirit into their bodies. The practice of receiving a spirit was inherited from the Boxers and resembles Boxer practices in all respects. The Boxer practices of eating cinnabar and inducing hyponosis are described in chapter two of my book, *Research on the Boxers.*

6. *Protection Against Bricks.* Red Spears members also practiced the smashing of bricks. After eating the ashes of an amulet and reciting a magic formula, society members would kneel on the ground and have bricks placed on their heads. Another member, perhaps a master, would swing a big metal hammer

at the bricks, smashing them. This ceremony was usually conducted at night, in an empty, heavily guarded courtyard, before an altar dedicated to the spirits. If by chance the bricks were not broken, the grand master would claim that the initiates were insincere or criminals.[12] Sometimes as many as five bricks were placed on an initiate's head. Actually, newly made bricks were fairly easy to smash without causing injury to the initiate, but the society members believed they were protected by the spirits.

When such a ceremony was in progress, nonmembers were forbidden to view it, but after the practice ended, it would be announced publicly to other members and to residents in the village that there would be a performance. Amid the blowing of horns, the beating of drums, and the clashing of cymbals, the master would describe the events to come. Then the society members would demonstrate their training for protection against swords and bullets.

7. *Protection Against Swords.* When rituals aimed at acquiring protection against swords were in progress, nonmembers were prohibited from watching; females especially were forbidden to look. It was said that if a female (the yin^a element) watched, the spirit would never descend into the male's body. Members who were to prticipate in the ceremony usually stripped to the waist, knelt before the altar, and ate the ashes of an amulet, shouting, "Begin the Teaching" [*shang-fa*]. They often recited a magic formula such as "Wu-liang Buddha protect my body; may the Two Guardians of the Gate protect me."[13] Then they each would place an arm on the altar, fist clenched. The person holding the sword would breathe deeply (this was called "holy breath" [*fa-ch'i*]), slowly breathe on the sharp blade, then would quickly swing his broadsword, stopping just short of the arms on the altar. A similar demonstration followed, directed against the stomach. The person who was to receive protection against swords would stand with two men holding each arm (or he himself would place his hands behind his back), with his mouth closed tightly and his stomach swelled with air. The member holding the sword would shout "Begin the teaching!" and would strike the other member's stomach three times with the sword blade. The skin of the stomach would turn red or deep purple from the blows.

The failure of the blade to cause injury to the stomach was not due to magic charms or protection by the spirits. Rather, it resulted from the special breathing of the society member and the swelling of the stomach with air. Almost anyone can do this who stops breathing when the blows fall and inflate the stomach. [In this state a person can] be hit by a sword without breaking the skin or drawing blood. But, the sharp edge of the blade also must fall at a precise perpendicular angle; otherwise it may cut the skin and seriously injure the stomach. I visited a former secret-society member from Shantung who had scars on his left wrist because once during a ceremony his master's hand had slipped.

8. *Protection from Guns.* Ceremonies to achieve protection against guns were held outdoors and many people would gather to witness them. The grand master would first select ten or so society members who, standing in a line and stripped to the waist, would eat the ashes of an amulet and recite a magic formula. About ten nonmembers, usually rich peasants or members of the gentry, would stand in another line holding modern rifles. Before loading, these rifles were examined by others. One of the gentry would fire into the air to prove that these were authentic weapons. Then the grand master would recite a magic formula and direct selected members of the society to rush toward the line of gentry. As they rushed forward, the gentry would aim at their chests and fire. The selected society members would shout such slogans as "The spirits protected us," "Guns cannot hurt us," and "We need not fear bandits." None of the men would be hurt by the bullets.

There was a bit of deception in this ceremony also. When the guns were loaded just before the men charged, bullets with wax heads would be inserted. That is why the grand master always chose members of the gentry to load and fire the guns; peasants would not question the verification of gentry members and the gentry often could not distinguish live ammunition from blank cartridges. The purpose of the ceremony was to strengthen the resolve of the members and at the same time frighten bandits. It was assumed that a member of a bandit gang was usually in the audience and would report to his cohorts the effectiveness of the secret-society magic. This is one reason why bandits often retreated in the face of Red Spears attacks.

Of course, Red Spears members were deeply convinced and believed firmly in the effectiveness of such rituals. A case was recorded in 1926 in which the forces of the warlord Wu Pei-fu were fighting the Shensi army. A Red Spears leader in Wu's forces was captured by the enemy. As he faced the gun that would kill him, he ate an amulet of ashes and patted his chest, saying, "Come on! Let's see if you can kill me!"[14] While many were killed in the ensuing battle, the grand master laid the blame on members, claiming that insincerity or failure to perform the rituals properly had prevented the spirits from descending into their bodies.

9. *Protection Against Cannon.* In the ceremony to achieve protection against cannon and artillery, the members were first led in worship at the altar by the grand master. Following this, the grand master would place an amulet inscribed in cinnabar red into a bowl of clear water and ask each man to drink.[15] Then the men would form a row about fifteen paces from the mouth of an old cannon and recite the magic formula for protection. The grand master would fire the cannon, which roared like thunder. The Red Spears members would be covered with gunpowder, but would not be hurt.

In this ceremony another trick was played by the grand master. He would first load the cannon with a small charge of gunpowder, then load the shell, then add more gunpowder. The shell was encased in the powder, which would explode as it left the barrel, but since the shell had almost no velocity it was harmless. If the shell happened to be loaded correctly, with a charge of powder behind it and none in front, some of the men might be killed. When this occurred the grand master would claim that the victims had been insincere or had conducted the rituals improperly.

Many onlookers believed what the grand master told them, but others did not accept these explanations. Such a case was recorded in 1926 in the village of Pai-shih-kang near K'ai-feng. In this village, during a ceremony to gain protection against cannon, more than ten Red Spears members were killed by the shell. The crowd of onlookers pounced on the grand master and beat him to death. A similar case was recorded in Shantung in 1928.[16]

In the final analysis, all the rituals of protection against swords, guns, and cannon involved some degree of deception.

Yet they raised the morale and confidence of Red Spears members tremendously, and gave them courage to advance fearlessly in battle.

10. *Protection Against Sickness.* Prior to 1941, superstitious practices in the treatment of illness were common in China's villages. Very few people were trained in Chinese medicine and even fairly large towns often lacked a doctor trained in Western medicine. When a peasant fell ill, the gods and spirits were called upon to cure him. Because the Red Spears society was known to have influence with powerful gods and spirits, peasants often went to Red Spears meeting halls asking for treatment. Most society branches had members into whose bodies a spirit had descended. These men, it was said, could cure the sick without medicine. When calling upon the spirits to cure a disease, rituals were conducted such as burning incense, asking a sprit to descend into the body of the victim, invoking the name of Buddha, and preparing magic charms which were dissolved and drunk by the sick person or hung above his bed or front gate. There were even red-colored "magic pills" [*hsien-tan*] which were believed capable of bringing the dead back to life.

Some of the ingredients in these magic pills may not have been medically helpful, they they were not harmful either. When administered, after a magic fomula was recited over them, the pills had the important psychological function of persuading the sick person to believe in their effectiveness. Thus, the sick might cure themselves as a result of the conviction that they were getting better.[17] After resting a few days and allowing the body to combat the illness naturally, peasants often would be cured, but credit for the recovery usually went to the spirts, amulets, and magic pills. Because of these experiences, peasant households automatically asked the spirits for help when sickness occurred and the fame of the magic treatments of the Red Spears grew. If a person died after the magic formulae were recited and charms applied, it was said to be the consequence of some sin on the part of the victim, a punishment by the spirits, or simply fate.

11. *Harnessing the Supernatural.* When a person became mentally ill, acting strangely, demanding certain objects, accusing others of harming him, and speaking incoherently, peasant households often called upon the Red Spears to send an exorcist. When the

exorcist came to the sick person's house, he would wash his own face and rinse his mouth, then burn incense and call on the spirits for help. He would find someone to sit quietly with his eyes closed; this was called "suspending sight" [kua-yen]. It was said that by first "suspending his sight," then opening his eyes the person became able to see the form of the devil who was tormenting the afflicted person.[18] Then he would tell the exorcist where the demon was located in the person's body.

It was not easy for the exorcist to determine the nature of the spirits which possessed a patient. Demons with violent or stubborn dispositions would cause the possessed person to act violently. First, the exorcists would berate the demons for haunting people. Sometimes, in order to drive out such a spirit, the "demon" (i.e., the afflicted person) was bound with rope and tapped between the eyes with a bundle of incense sticks. Some demons would cry out and leave the afflicted person, but others had to be drawn from the body and killed. The exorcist also might identify the number of demons and the portions of the body they were inhabiting. The most evil demons would be enticed into a jar. Then a magic charm would be placed over the mouth to seal it, and the jar thrown into a pond or a river. Soon the afflicted person would recover. Finally, it was necessary to call on other spirits to protect the patient, so incense would be burned on three or more succeeding days.

In many cases involving the psychological or emotional disorders described above, the afflicted person was a daughter-in-law in a traditional peasant household or a female family-member in poor health. Many women were physically weak and despite any emotional stress were forced to work hard. When they broke under such conditions the peasants considered them possessed by demons.

The exorcist engaged to drive out such spirits practiced a sort of hypnotism, causing the afflicted person to obey all his instructions. Other rituals of the exorcist, such as burning incense and calling the spirits, were empty, if mysterious, gestures, but they helped convince an afflicted person that the evil had been driven from him. Both approaches, hypnotism and rituals, were means of dealing with emotionally disturbed persons. Western medicine, although highly scientific, also uses these "psychological medicines" to treat emotionally disturbed patients, so one must recognize the efficacy of the methods used by the peasants in China.

12. *Worshipping the Broadsword.* Secret-society members who wished to change their ordinary swords into weapons that could force spirits and ghosts to retreat would undergo a ceremony called "worshipping the broadsword." The members first had to obtain permission to undergo the ceremony from the spirits through their representative, the grand master. A place known to be inhabited by spirits was selected and the society member would to there every night at midnight, no matter what the weather. The ceremony itself called for the member to hold a broadsword while reciting magic formulae. During that time the member could not see any other person and had to recite continuously. He had to do this on forty-nine successive nights before the ceremony was considered complete.

   Because this ceremony was so difficult, very few attempted it and many who began failed to complete it. One who completed the ceremony would never be possessed by an evil spirit. The self-discipline and perseverence required in this ceremony had an important effect on the entire society.

13. *Spinning the Table.* In this ceremony a bowl of water was placed on the ground and a table turned upside down and placed on it. With the legs of the table pointing skyward, four young boys would each grasp a leg with one finger. When the grand master, reciting a magic formula, said, "turn left," the boys would turn the table to the left; when he said, "turn right," they would turn the table to the right. The table would turn faster and faster as the boys ran in a circle, until they were told to stop. This was called "devils spin the table." Because a form of suction adhered the bowl to the table, it would not break and water would not spill. Moreover, forces created by the rotation of the table pushed the water down into the bowl, so that when the table was turned right side up again, it was perfectly dry. The onlookers would assume that these phenomena occurred on the orders of the spirits.

14. *Pushing the Cart.* In this ceremony a society member would strip to the waist and perform the ritual of eating the ashes of an amulet, reciting a magic formula, and doing some calisthentics. Then the tip of a red-tasseled spear would be placed against his stomach and the handle placed against a cart.[19] The member would advance slowly, pushing the cart

with the spear, but the tip of the spear would not break his skin. In this manner the cart might be pushed several meters. This ceremony was common in north China.

15. *Walking on Hot Coals.* First a patch of burning coals, perhaps ten feet long and three inches deep, would be prepared. Next the grand master would worship the spirits, eat the ashes of an amulet, and recite a magic formula. Then, barefoot, he would walk rapidly across the coals without being burnt. Often, however, before walking across the coals he would sprinkle them with salt, which would act as a cooling agent and decrease the strength of the fire. Peasants in China worked barefoot in the fields, and as a result the skin on the soles of their feet often thickened and lost its sensitivity. Some peasants developed the ability to stand on hot coals without injury. Others applied an oil to their feet which acted as an insulator. Some Red Spears members oiled the palms of their hands, which allowed them to grasp a hot iron rod without being burnt.

Today, in Taiwan, Hong Kong, and Singapore, it is fairly common to see mediums become possessed by spirits and walk across burning coals. One such occurrence, which took place in Taiwan on 5 September 1964, was recorded in some detail. The preparations were elaborate and began with the medium asking the heavenly spirits and gods for protection. In that ceremony more than two hundred persons walked across the coals, and one of them provided a detailed record of the magic chants and formulae.[20]

In the final analysis, all the magic practices of the Red Spears helped to raise the self-confidence of members by perpetuating the myth that they could not be injured by weapons. This contributed to the protection of their families and their homes. In battle, even in the midst of a rain of bullets, the Red Spears would advance steadily with complete faith in their superstitious rituals. In that sense these magic practices were the "soul" of the Red Spears.

Section 3: Amulets

Crediting amulets with magic charms and special powers, is a superstition that has existed in China for hundreds, if not thousands, of years. Its origins are obscure. Red Spears members regularly used amulets before battle to raise their morale and strengthen their resolve. Often they wrapped a cloth around their stomachs to protect them from injury. Members over twenty years of age wore red stomach-bands and those over thirty wore white stomach-bands, but in all cases the bands were made by the men themselves. Women were strictly forbidden to make them because the members believed a band made by a woman would be ineffective. Inside the stomach band was placed a magic charm, usually consisting of a piece of bleached linen inscribed with red characters. Another charm against injury, the "Protection of the Seven Stars" [*ch'i-hsing pi-lu-fu*] consisted of black characters written on a piece of red cloth.

Amulets meant to be burnt so the ashes could be mixed with water and eaten were always inscribed in cinnabar red on yellow paper. After the characters were written, the amulet would be ceremonially burned at the altar, the ashes crushed, and the resulting powder placed on the member's tongue. Other amulets were placed in a bowl of water, stirred until they dissolved or disintegrated, then drunk.[21] Some protected the body in general; others specifically protected against bullets.[22] Besides amulets to be placed in the stomach band or eaten, there were charms against illness which were placed on the gate of the member's house or over his bed. Often the specific form of the amulet varied according to the particular branch of the Red Spears.

Likewise there were numerous magic formulae which varied among the different branches of the Red Spears. Scholars have uncovered many such charms. For example, the formula to enter holiness simply consisted of invoking the names of three spirits: the Four Kings of Heaven, the Buddha, and the Five Storm Gods.[23] Others, such as the formula to protect against injury by a broadsword, involved calling on numerous spirits: "I humbly beseech the Spirits of the Five Stars [Chin-wu-shen] in heaven, and ask my ancestor to come down from heaven. May the gods, Star of the Right [Chang-ch'i] and the Guardian General drive away cannon shells. May the Duke of Chou seal the cannon barrel with peach blossoms; protect me, protect me, protect me, Buddha, Five Storm Gods, Wu-liang Spirit, and Five Gods of Lightning."[24] Many of these magical formulae asked for protection against bullets and swords.[25]

Human beings often are faced with occurrences that are difficult to explain.[26] In the relatively closed world of China's peasant villages, strange occurrences were credited to the activities of spirits, so magic charms and formulae were employed for control or protection. Such amulets and formulae came to play a very important role in the lives of many Chinese peasants. Although

urbane people might scorn such practices, they were accepted as
magical and powerful by Red Spears members and were common in
the small villages of the countryside. I remember such amulets
hanging in my village in Honan, when I was a child, and they were
accepted without question by Chinese peasants up to thirty or forty
years ago.[27]

Chapter V: Offshoots of the Red Spears

The Red Spears began as a single, unified organization. But, as its influence spread and the membership became more complex, the society began to evolve in several ways. Some branches, while still classified as Red Spears, adopted slightly different ritual practices. Each branch developed its own hierarchy and eventually some took different names. A number of these "offshoots" of the Red Spears are discussed below.

Section 1: The Yellow Spears Society

The Yellow Spears [Huang-ch'iang-hui] was an offshoot of the Red Spears which evolved from the Boxer Society. The Yellow Spears took its name from the yellow tassels that its members attached to their spears. It also was called the Yellow Gate Society [Huang-men]. Members worshipped the Jade Emperor in Heaven [Yü-huang ta-ti], also called the Heavenly Father [Lao-t'ien-yeh] or the Heavenly Way [T'ien-yeh-tao], as their founding spirit. Many of their beliefs and rituals resembled those of the Red Spears. They took as their slogan the words, "to uphold justice in the name of heaven, to avoid conflict and live in peace" [ch'u-pao an-liang t'i-t'ien hsing-tao].

Those who wished to join the Yellow Spears had to be recommended by a member. They would then enter the society's hall and worship before the spirits, telling why they wished to join and asking the spirits for permission to do so. After receiving permission from the society leader, who represented the spirits, they would undergo various rituals such as eating the ashes of three amulets,[1] learning the magic formulae and, before each meal, facing the sun and reciting a magic formula. Each evening after supper they would enter the meeting hall, wash their faces and hands, rinse their mouths, burn incense, and worship before the altar.[2] Often they

59

would ask the spirits if there was a special mission to be undertaken. They might spend one or two hours in the meeting hall every day.

A number of prohibitions had to be observed, for example, avoidance of sexual intercourse for one hundred days before a ceremony, and never facing south while urinating or defecating. In addition, certain foods such as garlic, onions, and mustard plants were forbidden.[3] Members of the society put yellow tassels on the tips of their spears and wrapped the handles of their swords with yellow cloth. When marching into battle they wore yellow outer garments. With all of the members dressed in yellow, an optical illusion was sometimes created in which their numbers seemed greater than was actually the case. The members believed themselves protected from knives and swords by their yellow clothing.

On one occasion, in the winter of 1929, a group of Yellow Spears fought a group of Red Spears in Hsin-tsan hsien in Honan. I witnessed this battle, which raged for two days. The Yellow Spears initially gained the upper hand but were defeated in the end. Over one thousand secret-society members participated and many were killed on both sides. I remember that some of those who were not wearing yellow clothing had yellow stomach bands on which magic characters were written. Five of my relatives were killed in the fighting.

Section 2: The Green Spears Society

The Green Spears [Lü-i-hui] was another offshoot of the Red Spears Society. It took its name from the green tassels the members affixed to their spears, and also was called the Green Tassels or the Green Gate. It began in Shantung but spread to other provinces, eventually becoming popular in southwestern Honan. The beliefs and rituals of the Green Spears differed very little from those of the Red Spears, but each member carried a piece of green cloth as his standard.[4]

Section 3: The White Spears Society

The White Spears [Pai-ch'iang-hui] naturally took its name from the white tassels its members attached to their weapons. It was also known as the White Tassels or the White Gate.[5] It was active throughout Shantung, Hopei, and Honan, and was strongest in the area of Chang-te in Honan.[6] The White Spears did not use such terms as "grand master," but in other ways resembled the Red Spears. It was basically a self-defense organization in which each major branch was headed by a member of the local gentry, and each village unit was headed by the village chief. The members wore ordinary clothing, but sometimes wrapped their heads in turbans of black cloth.

They worshipped the Emperor of the Northern Quarter [Pei-fang hsüan-t'ien ta-ti chen-wu] as their founder spirit. Besides this special deity, they worshipped all other spirits in the pantheon indiscriminately, and would always stop when they passed a temple.

At their initiation ceremony they would burn incense at the altar and arrange various preserved fruits there. The initiates would bow their heads four times, then kneel before the altar. The leader would hold three magic charms in his left hand,[7] and would place one of them in a bowl filled with water. He then would shake the bowl three times above the incense cauldron and with his right hand take a magic sword (said to represent the sword of the Spirit of the Seven Stars), and lay it on the ricebowl. While reciting a magic formula he would shake his head from left to right and blow three times at the bowl. Another magic charm was dissolved in the water and each initiate would drink one ricebowl of the water. The the leader would recite a magic formula and blow at the head, back, and front of each initiate. Finally, each aspiring member was given a piece of paper inscribed with a magic formula. After reciting the formula, the initiate was considered a full member of the society.

Among other prohibitions, members of the society had to abstain from sexual intercourse for forty-nine days after the initiation. Three times a day they faced the sun with hands folded and recited a magic formula three times, swallowing loudly after each recitation, and bowing their heads four times.

The White Spears Society was quite effective in maintaining order in the countryside and guarding against bandits. For example, in 1927 the warlord Chang Tsung-ch'ang was defeated in Shantung and escaped into Manchuria, but in the spring of 1928 he attempted to regain his lost territory. The local people were frightened and wanted to protect their homes, so the gentry in Tung-nan hsien formed a united organization among several villages and asked a thirty-two-year-old resident, Wang Ch'eng-chang, to found a branch of the White Spears. Three days after the branch was organized, a rival group of twenty or thirty people, calling themselves the Southern Army [Nan-chün], determined to destroy the new White Spears branch. The Southern Army gathered forty-two men armed with pistols and rifles (two were on horseback and one had a bicycle), but the group was defeated by the White Spears.[8]

Not long after, another local irregular army, commanded by a man named Wang Tzu-ch'eng, mobilized over two thousand men and began invading villages, confiscating horses and food. The White Spears organized more than thirty villages in the area and on the night of 12 June 1928 attacked the irregular forces, killing more than three hundred and dispersing the rest. As a result, the fame of the White Spears and their united village organization grew. In 1931 the area was victimized by a bandit named Liu Kuei-t'ang (nicknamed Black Seven Liu [Liu Ch'i-hei]), who headed a band of five to six thousand men. The White Spears mobilized more than five thousand people and drove Liu's band from the area. They then maintained law and order in the countryside.[9]

In 1937, when Japanese forces invaded north China, the White Spears was revived, not only to control bandits, but to attack the Japanese. A branch of the White Spears was very active in north China after 1946, but in 1949 they were destroyed.[10]

Section 4: The Black Spears Society

It was said that the Black Spears [Hei-ch'iang-hui], whose members tied black tassels to their weapons, was started by a man named Lu Yen-sha in Yang-wu hsien in Honan.[11] Although its beliefs and rituals resembled those of the Red Spears, the society evolved as an offshoot of the Boxers called the Black Boxer Society. Upon entering the society, initiates vowed to do whatever was demanded of them once they became members.[12] Before meeting an enemy in battle, they would eat the ashes of an amulet and recite a magic formula; their charms were said to be especially effective. After entering the society, members had to burn various types of amulets for one hundred days and practice every day with a sword. The Black Spears was founded in western Honan in 1925,[13] and by 1928 had spread throughout Honan, Hopei, and Shantung, claiming several hundred thousand members.

Section 5: The Big Sword Society

1. *Origins*

The Big Sword Society [Ta-tao-hui], which had its own special ritual practices, has a long history in China. It managed to survive despite frequent suppression by local officials. During the Sino-Japanese War of 1894, people in Shantung believed that the magic of this society could protect them from artillery shells. Many people practiced the group's rituals and its influence spread throughout the province.[14]

In May 1896, a Big Sword leader in Chiangsu province, P'ang San-chieh, came into conflict with a Christian church. P'ang wanted revenge and requested assistance from a Shantung Big Sword leader, Liu Shih-tuan. Liu sent more than one thousand men to destroy the churches in that area. They not only destroyed the churches, but plundered and fought with the government troops that finally suppressed them. It was reported that in June 1897, four or five hundred members of the Big Sword Society in the same area attacked a village church and burned many houses.[15]

In the following year German troops, claiming the need to protect German missionaries, occupied portions of Shantung province. As the Big Sword was proscribed by Chinese officials, its members began joining Boxer units in the area, adopting these antiforeign and anti-Christian views. Thus, many people assume incorrectly that the Boxers grew out of the Big Sword Society.[16]

After the Boxer Incident of 1900, the Boxer Society disbanded, but the Big Sword Society continued to exist secretly. In the spring of 1905 the Big Swords in Cheng-yang hsien in Honan planned an uprising against government officials in the area. The uprising was to include popular support and the date was set for 5 March. News of it was leaked, however, and it was suppressed by the *hsien* magistrate, Wang Kung-t'ang.[17]

As late as 1916, the Boxer Society was resurrected in some areas, calling itself the Red Spears Society. Because many of its members carried large swords, it also was known as the Big Sword Society.[18] The Big Swords were most active in Shantung, where they had over one million members.[19] They formed alliances with other secret societies, but in some villages all the young men joined the Big Swords.

Each member wrapped a red cloth around his head and wore a broadsword with a red cloth tied to the end of the handle. Each group had a red flag on which was written, "The Big Sword Society of X *hsien* X village." In the area where their influence was greatest even government forces dared not attack them.[20] From 1917 to 1931 they were strong in the coastal provinces of south-central China, Fukien and Chekiang. The rituals, beliefs, and magic practices of the Big Sword Society were so similar to those of the Red Spears that it is impossible to distinguish between them.[21]

2. The Big Sword Society in South Manchuria

In the autumn of 1927 several counties along the Ya-lu River in south Manchuria were troubled by bandit raids. The people decided to organize for self-defense under the leadership of some local gentry. The gentry decided to call on Yü Ch'ang-hai, a leader of the Big Sword Society in Shantung. He and several other men left Shantung and founded branches of the Big Swords in south Manchuria. Many local residents, having heard about the effectiveness of Big Sword charms against knives, joined the society and helped to resist the bandits. Soon the society had over ten thousand members in numerous *hsien*. The members were armed with spears and knives of all kinds and had a three-colored flag. The flag was white with a red border inscribed in black with the words, "The United Village Association" [Lien-ts'un-hui] of X *hsien*." By the end of that year the Big Sword Society was active in every *hsien* in the area and in each place the village headman or a member of the gentry was put in charge of the local branch of the society.[22] Of course, the master ranked above the branch leader and in that area all the most powerful masters, who acted also as inspectors in the society, were natives of Shantung between the ages of thirty-eight and forty-one.

The Big Swords grew so powerful in the area that the government ordered the society suppressed. The Big Swords in T'ung-hua hsien struck back on 2 January 1928 by attacking government troops and destroying telegraph lines. Soon joined by other branches of the society, they captured the county seat by 4 January. They were attacked by government (i.e., warlord) troops commanded by Wu Chün-sheng, border defense commissioner of the three northern provinces, and by Chi En-ming, bandit suppression commander of Fengtien province. The Big Swords were not easily defeated at first, so the government troops began a mass slaughter of all boys aged twelve years and above. With their raping, burning, and looting, the troops were as bad as the bandits had been. When the government campaign ended on 6 February, many members of the Big Swords escaped into the hills. The provincial government ordered the arrest of all society leaders in the area.[23]

Despite this, the society survived, and in April 1928 it again attacked government troops in Lin-chang hsien, suffering about fifty-seven casualties. In October a force of more than three hundred members of the Lin-chang Big Swords attacked a government patrol. At that time Lo Mei-chi, who commanded more than two thousand Big Sword members, was planning a large-scale uprising. Chang Tso-lin, the warlord in control of Manchuria, dispatched troops of the Thirtieth Fengtien Army to disperse Lo's men. After the Japanese invaded the area in 1931, the Big Sword Society in south Manchuria changed its name to the Red Spears Volunteer Army and became a patriotic force attacking the Japanese.

Section 6: The Iron Gate Society

The Iron Gate Society [T'ieh-kuan-chao] was an organization of young unmarried women. It evolved from the Red Lanterns [Hung-teng-chao], a group that had been affiliated with the Boxer Society. The purpose of this group was not to kill enemies, but to harass them and hamper their advance. Before a battle each Iron Gate member would hold a basket in her left hand (or would hold a basket in her right hand and a sword in her left), while reciting a magic formula. They believed this would cause bullets from the enemy guns to fall harmlessly into the baskets. The members of a similar group, which evolved from the Black Lanterns branch [Hei-teng-chao] of the Boxers, dressed in white and carried fans in one hand. With the fan each woman could cause enemy bullets to fall into a basket she held in her other hand. Because of this distinctive practice, the group was also known as the Basket Society [Lan-tzu-hui] and the Flower Basket Society [Hua-lan-hui].

Although there were a number of such groups scattered throughout the territory controlled by the Red Spears, most have escaped attention because they had relatively few members.

Section 7: The Spirit Soldiers Society

1. *Origin and Beliefs*

The Spirit Soldiers Society [Shen-ping] was organized in eastern Szechuan in 1925 by residents who sought protection against bandits and the depredations of warlord troops. It can be considered an offshoot of the Red Spears, with similar rituals such as eating the ashes of amulets and having spirits descend into the members' bodies. The name, "Spirit Soldiers," derived from these practices. They were also known as Heavenly Soldiers [T'ien-ping] and were said to practice the magical arts [*shen-shu*].

A report on the Spirit Soldiers appeared in the Shanghai *Central Daily News* in September 1928. The reporter had just returned from Ch'eng-tu and areas in Szechuan where the Spirit Soldiers were active. He reported that the territory of their greatest activity was the mountainous Wu-hsia region. Their original organization was said to have had just over one hundred people. Armed with spears and broadswords, they wrapped their heads in yellow turbans. By 1927 they controlled forty *hsien*, where no land or commodity taxes were paid to the government authorities. Due to their benevolent rule, membership grew to over one hundred thousand. Unarmed travellers were safe in their territory, but the warlord troops occasionally sent to suppress them met with fierce resistance.[24]

It is clear that the Spirit Soldiers opposed the bandits and warlord troops that plagued the area. They also resisted the heavy taxes that had motivated them to begin their protests.[25] These taxes and surtaxes were not the usual sort, but were excessive levies added almost at will by local warlords and government officials.[26]

By April 1928 the Spirit Soldiers had spread to northern Szechuan and neighboring Hupei. Bandits were especially troublesome in western Hupei after 1926 and local branches of the Spirit Soldiers were formed to resist. They believed they could make themselves invincible against bullets and swords, and even the educated residents accepted their claims.[27] They sometimes announced publicly that their goal was to protect themselves and live normal, peaceful lives.[28]

The Spirit Soldiers Society began as a peasant organization. But, like the Red Spears, its membership and programs grew more varied and complex. In addition to self-protection, it began to engage in tax protests and antibandit activities. Eventually some Spirit Soldiers advocated the assassination of local government leaders.

Some observers felt that the Chinese Communists encouraged the Spirit Soldiers to oppose local authorities.[29]

2. Organization

The Spirit Soldiers Society was a relatively complex organization. It was divided into six major branches known as the Heavenly Soldiers, Spirit Soldiers, Green Sword Society [Ch'ing-tao-hui], Big Sword Society, Single Sword Society [Tan-tao-hui], and Double Sword Society [Shuang-tao-hui]. They had a series of designations called "father" [ta-yeh], "second father" [erh-yeh], "third father" [san-yeh], and so on. They also had ranks such as unit commander [t'uan-chang], camp commander [ying-chang], and company and platoon commanders.

The Heavenly Soldiers dressed only in yellow, including their shirts, trousers, belts, and shoes. The Spirit Soldiers dressed in red, and the Green Swords in green. The Big Swords dressed in light green, the Single Swords in black, and the Double Swords in blue. The official color of the society was yellow, however, so in battle every member wore a yellow band around the middle finger of his left hand.[30] As their numbers increased, the organization grew even more complex with more official titles and special flags to distinguish each of their major commanders.[31]

3. Beliefs

The Spirit Soldiers looked back with longing upon the Ming dynasty, when the Chinese ruled China. They spoke disparagingly of the ruling Manchus and considered them an occupying enemy. They opposed any foreign presence in China, especially the foreign businesses that they felt exerted undue influence on the nation's affairs. They blamed foreigners for the overthrow of the Ch'ing dynasty and for subjecting China to their schools and policemen. They worshipped as a spirit the monkey who was a hero of the Chinese novel, *Jouney to the West* [Hsi-yu chi].

The antiforeign sentiments of the Spirit Soldiers were typical of traditional thought at the end of the Ch'ing dynasty, when many Chinese felt threatened by foreigners and rejected these influences. Nonetheless, the Spirit Soldiers were less aggressively antiforeign than the Boxers had been. Their belief in the monkey spirit is not surprising since the White Lotus Society [Pai-lien-chiao] once had been very popular in the same part of Szechuan province and had held strong Buddhist beliefs [*Journey to the West* concerns a voyage to India to obtain Buddhist scriptures]. It is understandable that the Spirit Soldiers were influenced by the White Lotus ideology, rituals, and beliefs. Unlike the White Lotus Society, however, the Spirit Soldiers were not intent upon seizing political power.[32]

Section 8: The Heavenly Gate Society

1. *Origins*

The Heavenly Gate Society [T'ien-men-hui] developed in northern Honan and southern Hopei around a man named Chang Kuo-hsin.[33] Their purpose was not, as some have claimed, to rob and pillage. Southern Hopei was a stronghold of the northern branch of the former White Lotus Society, and the Heavenly Gate Society was initially a branch of the White Lotus. The White Lotus Society was founded by Tung Szu-hai from Shantung province. Eventually the White Lotus divided into eight branches. During the reign of the Tao-kuang Emperor [1821-51] the eighth branch was established in and around Ku-ch'eng hsien in Hopei, calling itself the Fortunate Gate Society [T'ien-men-chiao].[34] Although severely suppressed by the government, the society continued in secret until the advent of the Republic, when it changed its name to the Heavenly Gate Society.

In 1925 the leader of the society in Lin-hsien in northern Honan, Chu Hung-teng, claimed to be a descendant of the last Ming ruler and proclaimed himself the new emperor of China. He was killed by government troops shortly thereafter, and that branch of the society was dispersed.[35] The Heavenly Gate Society often was confused with the White Lotus Society because of their similar origins and beliefs. Bandit excesses were severe in the area of Lin-hsien in 1926, and some forty residents revived the Heavenly Gate Society in order to protect themselves.[36] Claiming that their ritual practices would protect them from bullets, the society members elected as their leader Han Yü-ming, whose name could be construed as meaning "desiring the return of the Ming dynasty."[37]

In March 1926 the chief of the local self-defense forces, Li P'ei-ying, heard rumors that the Heavenly Gate Society had been reestablished. He took about ten men and went to investigate, but all were killed by the forces of Han Yü-ming. In early May Han's Heavenly Gate Society attacked a bandit gang headed by Ho Ch'ien-chin and took several hostages to hold for ransom. This

daring and successful raid spread Han's fame throughout the
surrounding countryside. As the society's membership grew in
numbers and reputation, Han's prestige increased as well. In his
home village of Yu-ts'un, Han erected a temple in honor of the God of
Literature called the Golden Bell Hall [Chin-luan-tien] where many
local people came to pray. In time the small village became a market
town. Soon nearby villages erected temples and began joining the
society. Their temples were filled with the sounds of ritual chanting.

Eventually Han Yü-ming came to be treated as a sacrosanct
leader with the power of life and death over society members. He
began acting strangely and caused many disturbances in the area.
In early July he attacked the county seat. The city's protectors were
armed with rifles and killed several society members, causing the
Heavenly Gate forces to lose momentum. On 30 July the city's
self-defense forces surrounded the Heavenly Gate troops but could
not overrun them. A few miles from Yu-ts'un the city forces were
defeated, and more than twenty self-defense men were killed or
captured. There was great commotion within the county seat and the
power of the Heavenly Gate Society increased tremendously. Even
the county magistrate was unable to suppress the society.[38]

2. Violent Activities

In the spring of 1927, branches of the Heavenly Gate Society
were established in the surrounding *hsien*. The society's power was
great and it engaged in skirmishes with other secret societies in the
area, sometimes winning and sometimes losing, but often suffering
fatalities. On 18 March 1927, some units of Chang Tso-lin's
Feng-tien Army attacked the Heavenly Gate Society in Lin-hsien,
forcing a retreat to An-yang. In June, the society's leader, Han
Yü-ming, entered the county seat of Lin-hsien and took up residence
in the Huang-hua Academy. He established eight administrative
offices, with such titles as general affairs, society affairs, financial
affairs, and legal affairs. He erected telephone poles and strung
wires, established an arsenal, and even sentenced some men to
death. Local residents were unable to curb his authority, and two
hsien magistrates, Chang Shih-chi and Liu Ch'i-yen, escaped from
the city under the cover of darkness. Han ordered two other
magistrates arrested and changed the names of their *hsien*.[39]

By autumn the membership of the Heavenly Gate Society in
Lin-hsien numbered several tens of thousands. The society attacked
a branch of the White Tassels Society in a village near the western

suburbs of Anyang and burned the village to the ground. On 16 August they attacked a nearby district and kept it under siege for a month, but were driven from the area by a unit of Feng Yü-hsiang's Kuo-min Army.[40] Several clashes between the Heavenly Gate Society and units of Chang Tso-lin's Feng-tien Army occurred in late December in Hopei's Tzu-hsien. The Feng-tien forces were forced to retreat. Ammunition and many weapons were captured by the society, which went on to plunder the coal mines in the *hsien*.

As their authority increased, extending as far as southern Hopei and western Shantung provinces, members of the Heavenly Gate Society often engaged in excessive violence. The recalcitrant and abrasive behavior of society members during that time was recorded in a song, "When you join the Heavenly Gate Society you will eat well and never mind the expense; you'll have fine shoes on your feet and wear your hair in a pigtail. With your mouth you will curse anyone, and you'll beat them with the handle of your spear; you will get into trouble in three days and be killed in five days. Your children will call another 'father,' and your wife will sleep with others."[41] As reflected in the song, members of the society acted as they pleased and enjoyed a rough existence.[42]

As the power of the Heavenly Gate Society increased, various warlords tried to use it for their own purposes. To gain the favor of Han Yü-ming, the Manchurian warlord, Chang Hsüeh-liang sent him an officier's sword. Han became an ally of the Feng-tien clique. The warlord Feng Yü-hsiang also wished to use the strength of the society, so he sent his staff aide Liu Wen-yen to meet with Han Yü-ming. Liu, however, was killed by Han's men. Feng was furious and in February 1928 dispatched two divisions to attack the society.

In the initial encounter, which lasted three days, Feng's divisions suffered many casualties but made little headway against the society forces. Han and his men withdrew to Lin-hsien. On 26 February Feng's troops entered the *hsien* and a two-day battle ensued. A group of Heavenly Gate units from neighboring *hsien* came to Han's rescue but were forced to retreat by the warlord troops. On 26 March Feng's commander was ordered to leave the *hsien* and proceed to An-yang where Feng-tien troops were attacking. He left one thousand men occupying the county seat of Lin-hsien, but a stalemate soon developed in which Han Yü-ming occupied the mountains west of the city and Feng's men occupied the county seat. This situation, in which bloody clashes occurred but neither side gained any ground, lasted for several months. Finally, in December 1928 Feng's forces attacked Han's mountain stronghold with the help of another warlord unit. Han's defenses crumbled, but he managed to escape to Feng-tien province in Manchuria.[43]

Han returned to defeat Feng's occupying division and reclaim his lost territory in March 1930. He began in the winter of 1929 by calling together his former commanders. They did not bother to erect an altar to the spirits, but concentrated instead on planning the defeat of Feng's division. Following his victory in March 1930, Han and his men, now the supreme power in the area, again marched into the county seat of Lin-hsien. The local garrison could not stop them and Han's men began occupying surrounding villages. Han renamed himself Han Fu-sheng, which means "Han the Reincarnated." In April he found himself again under attack by a warlord unit several miles west of the county seat. After several days of fighting the warlord troops were routed. Because of his supreme power in the region, Han was appointed a brigade commander by the Central government.

On 1 July 1930 Han reentered the county seat and formed an alliance with several bandit chieftans who commanded five to six thousand men. Each bandit gang was ordered to defend a portion of the surrounding area. These forces required millions of *yüan* each month for wages and provisions and pillaging and looting became daily occurrences in the villages where they were stationed. In 1931 even the county magistrate, Chou Ting, was forced to escape from the city under cover of darkness. Han's power was finally reduced in November 1931 when his bandit allies were executed by a newly appointed pacification commissioner, Liu Chen-hua.[44]

3. Organization

The Heavenly Gate Society was organized in a very dictatorial manner, so that all the power within the society was concentrated in the hands of Han Yü-ming. Before any mission was undertaken, the general unit master [*tsung-t'uan-shih*] would burn a magic charm written on yellow paper and ask instructions from the spirits. The instructions were in fact the orders of Han Yü-ming. Beneath the general unit master were the masters, who were responsible for either civil or military functions. The civil masters took charge of the erection of altars and various ritual matters, while the military masters dealt with combat and military matters.

The society had a total of about two hundred civil and military masters.[45] Only a master could erect an altar; thus, officially, only a master could establish a new branch of the society. If an altar was erected by an unauthorized person, the society would disband the illegal branch. Because of this tight control, the Heavenly Gate Society was a single and highly unified organization.

Many of the magic formulae and rituals used by the society were similar to those of the Red Spears. For example, the Heavenly Gate formula to gain protection against bullets read, "Open the heavenly gate, open the earthly gate, may the holy spirits come to us. Jade Emperor open the heavenly gate, ancient Buddha show us your holiness, hear our brothers reciting the magic formula. Stop the cannon from firing, stop all the cannons and guns from firing, silence the cannon and rifles."[46] Magic formulae to protect against injury were sought by the people whenever fighting increased in their locality. This occurred, for example, in Honan province in 1927, when fighting was heavy and more than 300,000 men between the ages of sixteen and forty-five were conscripted.[47] The Heavenly Gate Society held control over that portion of north China until 1931.

4. Defeat

Honan province experienced several difficulties in the late 1930s. After the Marco Polo Bridge Incident in July 1937, Japanese troops began occupying portions of the province. In the spring of 1938 crops were ruined by severe flooding in several *hsien*. Claiming that he wanted to pacify the area, a man named Hu Ch'üan-lu raised a band of five thousand men and began to collect food and forcibly requisition weapons.[48] His group turned to banditry, so a rich peasant named Yang Kuan-yi organized a branch of the Heavenly Gate Society for self-defense. Each participating village erected an altar, called the incense hall, and worshipped the society's standard deity, the God of Literature. In other respects this group was similar to the Red Spears; members were prohibited from sexual intercourse for three months following initiation, they gathered in the evenings for ritual practices, and so on.

The leader of their organization, the society commander [*tsung-hui-chang*] was Yang Kuan-yi. Beneath him were eight departments, including the staff department, the military supplies department, and the general affairs department. Members were assigned to units [*tui*], each large unit consisting of three middle-sized units, and each middle-sized unit made up of three small units. The small units averaged twenty to thirty members, while the large units had about five hundred. Each unit had a commander. In general their organization resembled that of a typical army. Their flags were blue with a yellow border and yellow characters, each giving the number of members in a particular unit. Their weapons were rifles and red-tasseled spears. Initially, officers and men wore blue uniforms, but later they switched to khaki to make themselves less visible to Japanese aircraft. Provisions were supplied by peasants in the surrounding countryside and, although pay was irregular and not fixed, each man received a ration of about two pecks of millet per month.

The Heavenly Gate Society of Yang Kuan-yi clashed with the forces of Hu Ch'üan-lu in the middle of April 1938, with heavy losses on both sides. Finally an agreement was arranged through local county magistrates, giving each organization a specific territory and forbidding fighting between them. The two groups did fight again in the summer of 1942, when Yang's Heavenly Gate Society, with over one hundred thousand men, drove Hu's forces out of the area.

During the Heavenly Gate uprising in 1938, the Chinese Communist Party sent a cadre named Hu Jih-ch'ing to join the society. He became a member of Yang's strategic staff. In July 1945 Yang was killed and the society was disbanded by the communists.

Section 9: The Limitless Society

1. *Ritual Practices and Beliefs*

The Limitless Society [Wu-chih-hui], also called the Absolute Society [T'ai-chi-tao], took its name from various concepts of Taoist philosophy and was active in southern Honan.[49] It began in 1912 in Shantung under a leader named Li Kuang-yen, who called himself the elder [*tsung-fang-chang*] and the literary master [*wen-shih*]. He claimed his magic could protect his followers against swords, bandits, and the demobilized troops who often pillaged the countryside.[50] Most of the people who joined the society were law-abiding citizens. They called their leaders "teachers" [*lao-shih*], called themselves "disciples," and among themselves used the term "society friends" [*hui-yu*]. The spirits worshipped by the society were Lao-tzu [T'ai-shang lao-chün] and other Taoist deities such as the Martial Emperor of Heaven [Hsüan-wu ta-ti] and the Great Martial General [Wu-kuang ta-ti].[51]

Besides such standard practices as dissolving amulets in water, conducting exercises with swords, and bathing in cold water,[52] special rituals were conducted by members known as "laborers" [*kung-fu-che*]. The laborers practiced breathing exercises after getting up in the morning and before retiring at night. In the morning they faced east to "welcome the sun," and in the evening they faced west to "send off the sun." With eyes closed and heads bowed, the laborers would recite the formula, "The center is limitless, and in the circle is the limitless way." They would inhale through the nose and exhale through the mouth, with the tongue slightly curled to channel the escaping air down the center of the mouth. At the same time they would rub their chests with their hands, which was supposed to strengthen their hearts. This exercise was repeated for one hundred days, after which it was believed sickness would be cured, the weak strengthened, the depressed made happy, and all problems satisfactorily resolved.[53] After mastering this exercise, it was said, an individual could safely roam the countryside at night, observe the bandits in their hiding places, and estimate the numbers of enemy troops.[54] Such a person was forbidden sexual intercourse and the meat of wild animals.

Although the society was organized for self-defense and only occasionally fought demobilized soldiers or bandits, there were times when it engaged in battle with armies. An incident of this sort occurred in October 1928 in Hsi-hsia hsien in Shantung province, when the head of the county police visited a village and demanded payment of three hundred *yüan* from the inhabitants, threatening to slaughter the entire population and their farm animals if his demands were not met.[55] The frightened villagers approached the teacher of the Limitless Society, who told them the time had come for the society to defend the people. He stated that, if any society member suffered injury, he would offer his own head as compensation.

The society selected thirty or forty boys from its youth section, who snuck into the camp where the head of the county police, his wife, concubine, children, and four bodyguards were sleeping. All were captured, taken to the north side of the village, and executed. Army troops were summoned, but the society launched a surprise attack against the newly arrived forces, killing several score. After three days of fighting, the warlord commander, Li Tao-ho, sent a telegram offering to negotiate a peace. The society replied that it was united with the people for protection against bandits, but it had no special quarrel with the government [i.e., provincial troops]. With the help of the local gentry a settlement was reached.

2. The Limitless Society in the War Against Japan

During the war against Japan, the Limitless Society was divided into two large branches. The first, in southern Shantung, operated in about eight *hsien* around Meng-yi hsien and was centered in the Liu Family Village. The head of the Liu clan was its leader. The second branch, in western Shantung, was headed by a man named Chang K'ung-wu. Chang's original name was Chang Chien-yang. A man of some intelligence and education, Chang had been an officer in various warlord armies and in the KMT National Revolutionary Army before becoming a monk in the Wu-t'ai Mountains and taking the holy name K'ung-wu in 1927.

After the Marco Polo Bridge Incident in 1937, Chang's mountain retreat was captured by the Japanese and he returned to his home village. Banditry was rife in the area that winter and Chang urged his fellow villagers to band together and protect themselves. Drawing upon the ideas of the Limitless Society, which were well known in the area, each village erected an altar and assembled in the evenings to burn incense. When bandits were sighted, the villagers would gather at the local temple for mutual protection.

In 1938 the society changed its name to the Central Way [Chung-yang-tao], which expressed its aim of supporting the Chinese KMT central government.[56] As a patriotic, anti-Japanese group, increasingly influenced by the KMT, the society adopted the numerals 3 and 5 as its insignia. The 3 represented Sun Yat-sen's Three Principles of the People and the 5 represented the KMT's five-powered constitution. In the winter of 1939 the Japanese began building blockhouses along all transportation routes. Under increasing Japanese surveillance, Chang changed the name of the group to the Happiness Way [K'uai-tao]. The society's magic formulae were kept strictly secret. Often Chang would disappear, then suddenly reappear in another place; it was whispered that he had become a living Buddha and that his followers had become monks.

The Limitless Society was also strong in at least thirty *hsien* in Honan. By 1940 membership in that province numbered over two million.[57] Although it did not have a single unified organization, it was effective in resisting the Japanese and in aiding Chinese government workers. In the summer of 1941 the group (then called the Happiness Society) launched attacks against Japanese occupation forces in Ts'ao-hsien. While casualties were suffered on both sides, the attacks resulted in the weakening of Japanese control over the area. In addition, the effectiveness of Chinese resistance was demonstrated to the local inhabitants. Chinese government personnel behind Japanese lines came to rely on the group for aid and usually made society temples their base of operations. Government workers would visit temples in the villages, proclaim themselves disciples of Chang K'ung-wu, and quickly receive assistance. However, the society clashed with Communist forces in Hopei in 1940 and the Communists published a book entitled *The Chinese Traitor, Chang K'ung-wu* [Han-chien t'ou-tzu Chang Kung-wu]. Fighting with Communist forces again erupted in 1945 and in 1949 the society was eradicated.[58]

Section 10: The Yellow Silk Society

The Yellow Silk Society [Huang-sha-hui] was an offshoot of the Red Spears. It claimed it could offer protection against cannon and was most active in western Shantung.

An existing record documents the protection of local residents from a bandit gang in June 1922.[59] When the KMT National Revolutionary Army entered the region in 1927, the Yellow Silk Society, which by that time had many branches was was quite active, organized a large meeting in Honan's Ch'üeh-shan hsien.[60] The society leader Chang Wen-hsüeh, delivered a speech praising the KMT Northern Expeditionary Forces for destroying such enemies of the people as the warlords Wu P'ei-fu, Chang Tso-lin, and Chang Tsung-chang. "Now that they have defeated Wu P'ei-fu," he went on, "we should seize our weapons and help them crush the other big warlords."[61]

The society began to dissolve after the completion of the Northern Expedition but was revived after the Japanese attack on north China. When fighting the Japanese, society members wore a stomach band with the eight trigrams and an amulet tucked inside. On 12 November 1938 an attack was launched against Japanese forces occupying the county seat of Hsia-chin hsien, Shantung province. The Yellow Silk Society, with three hundred men led by Yüeh En-p'u, and the Red Spears Society, with one hundred men led by Yü Feng-k'uei, attacked the Japanese at the eastern gate of the county seat at about 7:00 A.M. Two Japanese were killed while the secret societies suffered six killed and twenty wounded. The local people were impressed by the patriotic spirit of the secret societies.

In its ceremonies, organization, and ritual beliefs, the Yellow Silk Society was similar to the Red Spears Society.

Section 11: The Red Spears in Northeast China

The Red Spears in China's northeast differed in their beliefs and ritual practices from the Red Spears in China proper as a result of the special environment of Manchuria. Although the Red Spears appeared in the northeast as early as 1926 or 1927, established by migrants from Shantung province, the society was not active in the region at that time. The powerful warlord armies of the three provinces of Manchuria were expelled from the region by Japanese forces in 1931. Some former warlord generals, such as Ma Chan-shan in Hei-lung-chiang and Wan Fu-lin in Kirin, tried to establish independent governments in the northeastern corner of Manchuria.

Many Chinese miners and lumber workers lost their jobs after the Japanese invasion, so a native of Shantung named Grand Master Li [Li ta-fu-shih] founded a branch of the Red Spears among the workers of Pen-hsi, Fu-shun, and other industrial centers. Many citizens, including members of the old Big Sword Society, joined the new group. Several leaders in Hei-lung-chiang and Kirin, all natives of Shantung, became associated with the society. The members adopted a number of slogans such as "Protect the Nation, Guard the People, Safeguard our Homes," "Crush Japanese Imperialism," "Overthrow the Puppet State of Manchukuo," and "Chase Out the Japanese, Resurrect China." Because of heightened anti-Japanese feelings, the backgrounds of prospective members were checked to ensure that traitors would not infiltrate the Red Spears. If the check proved satisfactory and a sponsor was found, an individual was allowed to join the society.

Prospective members were expected to refrain from sexual intercourse for one hundred days prior to their initiation. This prohibition usually was not enforced after the initiation. Initiations took place at the beginning of each lunar month, usually in the evening. There could be as few as ten or as many as several hundred initiates. During the ceremonies, each aspiring member would write in red cinnabar on a yellow paper the names of his ancestors for three generations and his own date of birth. The initiates would kneel before the altar and eat the ashes of an amulet, then the paper would be burned and the spirits asked to receive it. The grand master would chant, "May your eyes not see this world, may your ears not hear loose talk. Do not steal, do not insult your ancestors. Above, keep secrecy to your parents; in the middle, keep secrecy to your brothers; below, keep secrecy to your wife. If you disregard these instructions, may the Heavenly Emperor not protect you!"

Next, a white cock would be killed (sometimes black or red cocks were substituted) and the blood offered to the spirits. The grand master would chant, "Our Ancestors, I bow to you; Buddha with great holiness and great energy, help us to be strong. Our brothers, I bow to you; Buddha with great holiness and great energy help us to be strong." Each time the grand master repeated, "I bow to you," he would bow to the floor in a kowtow with his hands together. His hands were not allowed to touch the floor. Then, with his left hand placed on his right, he would bring both hands to the top of his head and kowtow. This was called the "five hearts," composed of two hearts in the hands, two in the feet, and one in the head. At the conclusion of the ceremony the initiates would ask to receive the teachings of the Red Spears and would eat the ashes of an amulet. The amulet was placed on the thumb and wrapped around the index, ring, and little fingers (with palms turned outward). The grand master would chant, "Save us White Lotus, Save us Shining Lantern, Save us Precious Sword; May the White Lotus bloom all over the earth, May Lao-tzu, whom we petition, give us his teaching. Compassionate Ancestors, Compassionate Masters, Our Worshipful Emperor, Command This." Finally, the grand master would whisper the special formula, "Metal, Rocks, and Stars approach to help us worship the Buddha."

Those who received the teaching would recite the special formula, very quickly and with closed mouths. Once the impact was felt, initiates often acted strangely, clapping their hands, jumping about, and making odd noises. When an initiate did not react in this manner, the grand master would recite another formula: "The sun, moon, and stars above the head, the water, fire, and wind beneath the feet, the body covered with thousands of lotus flowers. This brother has asked the spirits for help. Compassionate Ancestors, Compassionate Masters, this brother has asked; Our worshipful Emperor in heaven, command this." While the master recited this formula, a magic charm was wrapped around the finger of the initiate, and he would receive the teaching.

After about half an hour, the time would come to end the ceremony by "sending off the holiness" [sung-fa]. Once again, magic formulae were recited, including the chant that had been spoken after the killing of the cock. In the beginning no weapons were used in the ceremony but later they were included, with the grand master placing a red tassel on each member's spear. This ceremony was known as "receiving the spears" [*shou-ch'iang*]. After receiving the spears and exhorting the spirits to protect them, the initiates became full-fledged members of the Red Spears.

1. *Organization*

The great holy master [*ta-fa-shih*] was the most revered leader of the Red Spears in northeast China. Beneath him was the grand master, then the group known as the "holy youth" [*fa-t'ung*] who were organized in divisions of ten. Finally there were the society members. Within these divisions the society was organized along military lines. The grand master was sometimes called the commander [*szu-ling*] or bridge commander [*lü-chang*]; beneath him were units [*t'uan*], camps, companies, and platoons. As for weapons, the grand master carried a sabre, the master carried a broadsword, and members used red-tasseled spears or modern rifles.

All members were subject to strict discipline. Rape was punishable by death. Other crimes such as robbery or disrespect toward parents were given varying degrees of punishment, including loss of an ear or expulsion for the society.

Members' clothing always had protective charms or sayings written on it. This clothing was usually black with red characters inscribed with phrases such as "Buddha of Fate" [Yün-liang fu-ho]. On the left side of the front of a garment were written the characters for the Six Feminine Gods and Six Masculine Gods [Liu-ting liu-chia], which referred to the basic elements in astrological calculations. Beneath was the name of the society members. Inside the clothing was a picture of a deity such as the Sakyamuni Buddha, the Milo Buddha, or Lao-tzu, painted on white silk. Sometimes the names of these deities were written in place of a picture.[62] On the back of the garment was a phrase such as "Buddha of Fate" and to the upper left the words, "The Branches and Stems, Open the Hills" [*ting-chia k'ai-shan*]. Again the individual's name was written beneath. A picture of another deity, sometimes the Goddess of Mercy, would be painted inside a black panel.

Society members were subject to certain ritual prohibitions such as avoidance of sexual intercourse for three days before combat. They were forbidden to enter a lying-in room where a woman had just given birth and could not take their magic amulets into an outhouse. Those were known as the three forbidden rooms. Certain foods were also proscribed, for example, the meat of beasts of burden, including camel, dog, horse, and cow; and certain seafoods, including eel, shrimp, and loach fish.

2. Ritual Practices

In many respects the rituals of the Red Spears in Manchuria were similar to those of the society in China proper but, perhaps because of climatic extremes and the frontier spirit in the northeast, this offshoot developed some frightening rituals of its own. Because some of these evolved from Manchurian shamanism, a discussion of popular religious practices will aid in understanding the rituals of the local Red Spears.

Shamans and sorcerers in Manchuria believed they could control and do combat with spirits. Sometimes spirits were called upon, after appropriate sacrifices and rituals, to cure an afflicted person. At other times a spirit would cause a possessed person to dance and run about. In their spirit rituals the shamans themselves would perform wild dances, sing loudly, and exhibit other sorts of strange behavior. Having seen these shamans in action, the Red Spears adopted some of their magic practices.

In one ritual, called "walking on the ploughshare," the blade of an ordinary plowshare would be heated until it was red hot. Then vinegar would be smeared on the soles of a member's feet and he would run across the glowing blade unharmed. The people believed that magic protected the society member from harm. A similar ritual was called "salvaging a coin from a pan." First, a cooking pan was heated until it glowed red, then a crock of cooking oil was poured into the pan. A society member would suddenly reach into the pan and scoop up a coin that had been placed on the bottom. The member was able to do this because the addition of the cooking oil lowered the temperature of the pan, but the people believed that the magic of the spirits protected him from burning. In a ritual called "riding on the sword blade," a large knife of the sort used to cut grain was held by two persons, with the edge pointed upward. The grand master would stand on the edge without being cut.

These were some of the more impressive rituals adopted from the shamans of Manchuria. Other Red Spears rituals common in Manchuria were variants of those conducted in China proper. All of them had a strong impact on the people who watched.

3. Destruction of the Red Spears in Manchuria

When the Manchurian Red Spears launched an attack they preferred to do it in the dead of night. They disguised themselves as firewood peddlers and inside their bundles they would hide spears, rifles, and ammunition. Those who infiltrated towns in this manner were sometimes called the Dare to Die Corps. At an appointed time the disguised Red Spears members would begin to assemble and a fire would be lit to signal the beginning of the attack. The sleeping enemy would be caught off guard. The Japanese forces occupying Manchuria suffered many casualties in this manner. One entire encampment of Japanese troops in Hei-lung-chiang's Wang-kuei hsien was annihilated and over one thousand Japanese troops were killed in Kirin's Pai-li hsien, although in that attack the Red Spears lost three thousand men. In response to these attacks, the Japanese began using heavy weapons to defend themselves and disperse the Red Spears.

Many Red Spears members joined the Chinese resistance, called the Volunteer Army [I-yung-chün]. A Red Spears leader named Yü held power in the area of Pao-ch'ing hsien in Kirin, but the independence of the Red Spears members sometimes caused fighting to break out between the society and the Volunteer Army. One such incident in April 1937 involved the Eighth Volunteer Army, headed by Hsieh Wen-tung and a self-defense unit headed by Li T'ien-ch'ih. When one of Li's officers was killed in the fighting, the army attacked Yü's Red Spears. After heavy casualties on both sides, they negotiated a truce in light of the shared goal of resistance to Japan.

In battle the grand master often remained in the rear, though sometimes he led the ranks, shouting, "The rifle bullets cannot pierce us, the cannon balls cannot enter our bodies, the knife blade will not cut us, arrows will now hurt us. Forward!" On the cry of "Forward!" [t'iao] the society members would advance; if the grand master shouted "Kill" [sha] they would halt. Eventually Yü's Red Spears units were absorbed into the Third Volunteer Army headed by Chao Shang-chih. The two other major Red Spears units in Manchuria likewise were incorporated into the Chinese resistance forces: the unit headed by a man named Tu became part of the Eighth Volunteer Army and the unit headed by grand master Li joined the First Volunteer Army of Yang Chen-yü. Later both the Red Spears and the Chinese resistance forces were crushed by the Japanese occupation troops.

Section 12: The United Village Society

Because Red Spears branches often were organized among several villages, they were sometimes mistakenly referred to as the United Village Society [Lien-chuang-hui]. In fact, although both the Red Spears and the United Village Society were organizations designed for mutual protection, they were different in other ways. Their organizational structures in particular were quite dissimilar.

The United Village Society had its beginnings in the middle 1800s during the Nien Rebellion in northern China. Because government forces were inadequate to meet the threat of the rebels, villages were forced to unite for their own protection.[63] The society also was active around the time of the Boxer Rebellion in 1900 and was resurrected once again when warlord brigandry became rampant in north China after 1918.

In the early twentieth century groups met only when danger threatened. They were often called together by local gentry, then dispersed when the danger had passed; they had no formal organization to speak of. The first formal organizational structure developed in Shantung province around 1928, when United Village Society units posted regular guards in their villages, even when there was no immediate danger. Later they hired men to act as a security or police force. Every village had its own force, called a *t'uan*, every ten or so villages formed a flank [*tuan*], and every ten or so flanks constituted a society [*hui*]. Each unit had its own commander who was responsible for training and for general affairs. Each village had its own pay scale and households with sons in the force were assured of protection.

The provincial government of Shantung attempted to alter the organization of the United Society in the spring of 1929. At that time officials announced that the society would be known thereafter as a self-defense force [*pao-wei t'uan*] with the county magistrate as its commander.[64] In 1930 the society was reorganized and each *hsien* was ordered to form a united village group. According to articles 2 and 3 of the new order, each village was to form a branch and all the branches in a *hsien* would comprise one general society [*tsung-hui*] with the county magistrate at its head. The society was subdivided into districts and townships according to the normal administrative divisions within the *hsien*. All men between the ages of twenty and forty were required to enroll in the society regardless of their financial status or position within the *hsien*. All were required to follow the society's regulations and serve on active duty. Within

Shantung's Hsia-chin hsien the regulations stipulated that each household with twenty to thirty *mou* of land would provide one man to the society, those with fifty to sixty *mou* would provide two men, and those with sixty to one hundred *mou* would provide three men.[65]

This form of organization, with self-defense units established at all administrative levels, gave great impetus to the struggle to meet the goal of self-defense.[66] Expenditures for each society branch were about twenty *yüan* per month; the money was provided by the *hsien* government from public funds.[67] Weapons were supplied by the people themselves, so that the number and kind of weapons available differed greatly. Initially, in Hsia-ching hsien, for example, regulations stipulated that persons owning thirty *mou* of land had to provide one rifle to the society. Later the number was increased, so that eventually even those with less than thirty *mou* had to provide handmade guns.[68] Regulations in Tung-p'ing hsien required owners of twenty *mou* of land to provide one handmade gun and those with fifty *mou* or more to provide one rifle. Owners of one hundred or more *mou* were expected to provide even more.[69]

A record of the weapons and ammunition held by the United Village Society in Kuan-t'ao hsien gives some idea of the size of the organization. Within the *hsien* the society had 4,061 members. Besides large quantities of knives and swords, it had 1,817 rifles with 89,300 rounds of ammunition; 1,913 handguns with about 9,900 rounds of ammunition; 415 muskets with 24,000 musket balls; and 1,522 spears.[70]

To encourage public interest in the united village concept, the government published a song for the United Village Society: "Watching and protecting each other, we have organized to show our own strength. United villages, united villages, with one heart and our combined strength we guard against bandits. Protecting our homes, safeguarding our countryside. We will not be frightened, we will not run away. Protecting ourselves with our own strength, advancing into battle bravely grasping our long spears. Now our homes and families will be peaceful and strong together."[71]

Each society officer was responsible for guarding against fire or bandits and for reporting to his superiors and neighboring commanders in case of trouble. Probably the clearest organizational chart could be compiled for Shantung's Kuan-t'ao hsien, where there are records of the districts encompassed by each of the eight societies of the *hsien* and lists of the names, ages, and administrative positions of each of the eight society commanders.[72]

In 1930 all *hsien* in Shantung were ordered to cooperate with the United Village Society and bring them up to full strength. Since both rich and poor were expected to bear the burden, there was opposition among the people, especially the poor, who composed a song which voiced their criticisms of the society. The song described a group of peasants working hard in the fields who were called away to bear arms for the society. When they returned home not only were their fields untended, but they were expected to provide money and supplies to the society.[73] Despite this opposition from the poor, however, the peasants in general supported the concept of the society, which protected them from bandits.

Perhaps the most effective group was the United Village Society in Shantung's Hsia-chin hsien, which in late October 1931 defeated a bandit gang after a battle which lasted a day and a night. On 24 January 1932 the county magistrate ordered the society of Su-hsien to route sixty bandits, led by Wang Chih-ch'i, who had barricaded themselves in an old tower. From April to September the society commanded by magistrate Hsieh fought bandit gangs which at times numbered up to one thousand men, defeating them in every case.[74]

In 1934 each *hsien* in Shantung was ordered to establish a school for the training of members of the United Village Society. Each school provided a three-month course and generally enrolled forty to sixty members at a time. The first courses were completed in June 1934. The length of each class was later extended to four months.[75] In May 1935 Chi-tung hsien opened a school at the county seat which was supervised by the county magistrate. Its training course was offered every three months. In August 1935 all districts [*ch'u*] were ordered to appoint their own chief officers to lead the members in self-defense drills.[76] The United Village Society in Shantung remained active until the Japanese invasion of north China in 1937. During the occupation many society members performed heroic deeds as part of the Chinese resistance.

Section 13: Other Societies

A great number of other secret societies were active in the countryside during the twentieth century. Many were influenced by the Red Spears Society, even when they had no official connection with it. Some of these groups have been mistaken for branches of the Red Spears. Though all of them differed to greater or lesser degrees, every group was based on the idea of an organized mutually cooperative society.[77] Some of the minor societies are discussed below.

1. *The Small Sword Society*

The Small Sword Society [Hsiao-tao-hui] of north China was an offshoot of the Big Sword Society and its rituals and beliefs were similar to those of the parent organization.[78] The society was most active in the northern Anhui counties of Feng-yang hsien, Lu-chou hsien, and Shou-chou hsien, and in northern Kiangsu province. An uprising of the society occurred in Su-ch'ien hsien, northern Kiangsu, on 13 February 1929, when the KMT tried to suppress superstitious activities. The society used such slogans as "Crush the Three Principles of the People" and "Eradicate the Local KMT Office." It was led by a former Ch'ing dynasty degree-holder [*hsiu-ts'ai*]. In this uprising the Small Swords mustered up to forty thousand modern repeating rifles (in addition to their red-tasseled spears) and mobilized about fifty thousand followers.[79]

2. *The Fan Society*

The Fan Society [Shan-tzu-hui] was active in Honan province. It was led by a man named Chang Feng-tzu ["Crazy Chang"] who claimed to have learned his magic from a celestial being. In this group possession of a magic fan and eating the ashes of an amulet were supposed to protect a member against bullets. Initiates were given a paper fan and magic amulets. Various magic characters were written on the fan.[80] In addition there were spirit fans, spirit swords, the Eight Diagrams, and so forth, to protect a member against bullets.[81]

Many cases of looting and robbery by the society members were reported in 1917, 1918, and 1919. In 1938 the group was opposed by the Yellow Spears Society in Yen-chin hsien after some members of the Fan Society began confiscating grain and other food. Led by Chang Tzu-heng, and carrying yellow-tasseled spears and short swords, the Yellow Spears units defeated the Fan Society.

3. *The Mysterious Way Society*

The Mysterious Way Society [Miao-tao-hui[a]], also known as the Temple Society [Miao-tao-hui[b]], claimed that its members could cure illness through their ritual practices. They often engaged in robbery. Their leader was a man named Chu Chin-k'ang, from Honan province. The society was very active on both sides of the Yellow River.

In 1928 the Honan provincial government outlawed Buddhism and ordered its images destroyed. The society retaliated with an uprising against the local authorities in March. Members wrapped their arms with yellow cloth and called themselves the Central Self-Government Army [Chung-yang tzu-chih-chün], proclaiming the first year of the Great Han Republic. Several branches of the society in neighboring hsien responded to the call for revolt.[82] During the first ten days of March, over one thousand members, led by Hu Kuei and Chang Ch'en, conducted an unsuccessful seige against Yu-hsien. Following this defeat the society united with local bandit leaders Ch'ai Fu-chih, Wang Fu-ch'ing, and Nan Hua-wen to form a group called the Way of the Black Tiger [Hei-hu-tao]. The combined forces plundered about seventy villages.[83]

In April the Mysterious Way Society attacked several other hsien and killed many people. They then attacked the county arsenal but were routed by an army commander, Ch'en Te-hsing. After that failure, most branches of the society were suppressed and many members were driven from the area.[84]

In pursuing the relevant materials, one can easily find the names of numerous secret societies; my research has uncovered thirty-nine such groups in addition to those discussed above. It is often difficult or impossible to gather much information about the smaller groups. Some of them, it appears, were haphazardly structured and may have disbanded quickly. Others were better organized but were strictly local and did not have widespread influence. This chapter has reviewed the major offshoots of the Red Spears (all of which were influenced by it) as well as some societies that were confused with the Red Spears. The thirty-nine smaller secret societies whose names I uncovered were not connected in any way with the Red Spears, even though it appears that some of their ritual practices were similar.

Chapter VI: Transformation of the Red Spears

In the beginning the Red Spears was basically a local militia organized by peasants for self-defense. The various units were given the task of guarding villages against bandits, protecting homes and property, and generally providing assistance to local residents. As the Red Spears developed, its character changed. It grew in strength and became a more complex organization. It was used by factions, such as rich landlords, landless peasants, and bandit gangs. Aspects of the Red Spears as a complex organization are explored below.

Section 1: Tax Protests

The goal of the warlords was to conquer and occupy territory. They harrassed the common people, who suffered under their domination. Under their occupation, the people sometimes found the strength to protest against unfair taxation, especially against taxes imposed by the warlords.

For example, the general headquarters of the Red Spears in Honan issued a proclamation to the people of K'ai-feng (referring to it by its old name, Pien-liang) stating the reasons for a tax protest against the warlords. The proclamation read,

> People of K'ai-feng! When Wu P'ei-fu arrived in Honan last year he agreed that for a period of three years he would not collect land taxes and would abolish various minor taxes. Although he has been in Honan for a year, he has not ceased collection of the land tax or abolished minor taxes. Taxes have increased tenfold since he came. Recall that before he came we risked our lives against swords and fire, and so he came to pacify the province. Now our sufferings are worse than when the Second Division (composed of Shensi troops) was stationed here. This levy, that tax, today this request, tomorrow that demand; we

have to sell our grain and pawn our clothing, and still it is not enough to pay his goddamn taxes.

See for yourselves that the troops are worse than the bandits. When the troops encounter a bandit gang they pay no attention and it is we who must suffer. Brothers of Honan, the brothers of Hsin-an, I-yang, Lo-ning, Teng-feng, and Yen-shih have already raised their fists and begun a tax protest. We brothers in every *hsien* of the province are prepared to join them.

Compatriots! The difficulties Wu P'ei-fu is causing in the city are no worse than the difficulties he is causing in the countryside. Where will you borrow money to pay the special month's rent tax or the special kerosene tax? In addition to auctioning the outlying districts for five *li* surrounding the city, Wu has printed five million *yüan* of paper bank notes issued through the Silk and Tea Bank and is enforcing their use. Rest assured, he wants your life and he is not going to stop until all businesses, large and small, fall into bankruptcy. Will you endure this? After so many years in business, will you now close your doors? You can dare to rise up and rebel. We, your brothers in the countryside, want to help you. People of the city of K'ai-feng! Falling down is one kind of death but you can also die of living when forced to pay high taxes. It is the same as dying at the hands of police and *yamen* officials. But, if you bring glory to yourselves, we can truly call you men of Han. Future generations will not want to hear that troops were summoned or that the officials placated you with honeyed words. Because the officials are treacherous, we have only ourselves to rely upon. We must unite among ourselves and then we will fear nothing.

Compatriots, rise up! We, your brothers in the countryside, have vowed to help you. Oppose the forced collection of the extra month's rent tax, oppose the special tax on kerosene, oppose the auctioning of city land, oppose the use of Wu's paper script, burn the Silk and Tea Bank, crush Wu P'ei-fu! Unite with one heart and dare to rise!"[1]

From this text, one can see that the people's tax protests were the result of warlord excesses and were not directed against the legitimate government. There is a view that the Chinese are among the best of the world's people. This is explained as due first to the fact that in the past they had no special, individually held, political ideology and no special ambitions toward government; and, second, because the Chinese, with many poor people, natural calamities, and famine, learned to accept the vagaries of fate. Rather than accept hunger and cold, or mortgage their houses, or rush to meet official demands,[2] the people had a saying that expressed their sarcasm: "After you have paid your taxes, you will enjoy unrestricted leisure" [i.e., you will have nothing left].[3] It was no use, they realized, asking officials for protection.

When living became unbearable and a full-scale uprising was impossible, the peasants initiated more limited protest movements. They protested against the special taxes they considered unfair, but paid their normal taxes as before. An announcement from Szechuan read as follows:

> Notice to the people. We have learned that the officials at the Meat and Wine Tax Collection Office only beat and harass the people, causing much suffering among them. There seems to be no recourse and no one intends to rescind these taxes and levies. When the taxes are forcibly collected, some people do not have enough to eat. In collecting the taxes, proper receipts are not issued. Even when these are private levies imposed upon us, the officials who collect them are protected by the law.
>
> In the future, if troops are sent to the countryside to collect these private taxes, report it to us and refuse to pay the tax! Our unit will deal with those who harrass the people. Those who cause difficulties can be reported to our regional units or to our leader here. After we have arrived, all the people will know that the old unfair taxes of the Great Ch'ing dynasty do not accord with people's rights. There are only the emperor's taxes and no other legitimate levies. The people must recognize that the old Ch'ing taxes are not in force. They should instead follow the law of the Republic.[4]

The so-called emperor's taxes referred to the land tax, which was seen as legitimate, while other miscellaneous levies were not. The people were willing to pay legitimate taxes. However, they were unwilling to pay those they considered unfair, saying that the people now had rights. The warlords and politicians objected to this, as can be seen in the records of the protest movements in many localities.

In the summer of 1925 a riot broke out in Chi-tze hsien in Chihli province. The cause of the riot was a special tax, over and above the land tax, which was to be retained and used within the *hsien*. Local officials collected that tax and apparently divided it among themselves. The sum collected in the special levy surpassed the amount collected in regular land tax. Finally the peasants could bear it no longer. The local Red Spears and Yellow Spears joined the Red Spears in the western part of the *hsien*. The western Red Spears were led by a man named Yin,[b] and those in the eastern section were led by a man named Chin. Together they led the masses into the city, where a riot erupted. The headquarters of the *hsien* government was destroyed and many officials, including the chief secretary and the county magistrate, Li Kung-t'sai, fled in fear.[5]

At the same time, tax protests were initiated in many *hsien* to the south. In Tung-ch'i hsien, in 1926 hundreds of Red Spears members, led by Lou Pai-hsün, protested taxes in all parts of the *hsien*. The superintendent of the Honan Provincial Army, K'ou Ying-chieh, dispatched troops to the area, where they burned hundreds of villages[6] and killed four or five thousand people, including women and children, the old, the sick, and the young. They also confiscated grain and abducted young girls.[7] Similar cases of tax protests can be found, many of them recorded in *hsien* gazetteers.

Section 2: Protests Against Warlord Troops

When the Red Spears was founded, its basic purpose was to guard against bandits and protect homes. The society did not accept army deserters[8] and did not consider the government's military forces as it enemy.[9] When the warlords began assembling irregular armies, their forces often had no weapons.[10] Some were insufficiently paid or not paid at all.[11] These forces were ineffective against bandits and could not alleviate the sufferings of the people. Soon the warlord troops made no distinction between the people and the bandits and the peasants came to hate the soldiers. Thus, bad relations developed between the Red Spears and the military.[12]

A number of cases are recorded of bitter relations between the Red Spears and warlord troops. For example, when Yüeh Wei-chün was governor of Honan, he sent troops from Shensi to rule the province. Their attacks were violent and the people, who suffered greatly, developed a deep hatred for Yüeh.[13] Acting on that hatred, in the spring of 1926 the Red Spears organized several thousand people in western Honan. Over ten thousand Shensi troops threw down their weapons when attacked by the militia[14] and their forces were destroyed. At the same time, the Red Spears units in several Shantung *hsien* rose up to avenge the killings by warlord troops. In response, a bridge commander of Shantung troops, Fang Ch'ang, led his forces to an attempt to exterminate the Red Spears. He stationed his troops at Tung-p'ing, where they requisitioned houses and confiscated grain. The troops ordered most of the trees cut down outside the city wall and occupied the city from spring until winter. The people suffered bitterly, expressing their plight in a popular song: "The people cannot go about their business, their lives are disrupted. Their grain is seized and they must fell trees. The oppressed people dare say nothing, they bear it without a word. Nonetheless, they know their plight, for their eyes can see."[15]

In the fall of 1926 fighting broke out between troops and the Red Spears at Te-hsien. A bridge commander of the government forces in nearby Lin-hsien, Ho Wen-liang, led some troops into the area, intending to station them there. The Red Spears, thinking this was an attack, encountered Ho's troops in a village north of the city and killed a score of them. In anger, Ho ordered his forces to plunder and burn an entire village in the vicinity.[16] In the winter of 1926 the Heavenly Gate Society attacked Feng-tien troops in many *hsien* in the Tz'u-chou area of Hopei and in the An-yang area of Honan.[17] In the spring of 1927 the Red Spears fought in several *hsien*, including Hsin-yang, Cheng-yang, Hsi-hsien, Ch'üeh-shan, and Lo-shan, against troops led by Wei Yi-san, called the Picked Troops of the Wei Unit of the Ever Victorious Army [Ch'ang-sheng-chün]. The action took place during February and March. Large cannon were used and several thousand men participated on each side. The battle is recorded in some detail in the gazetteer for Hsin-yang hsien. The army was defeated completely.[18]

At the same time, a unit of the Honan Army was occupying Huang-chuan, the soldiers claiming that they would destroy the Red Spears. These troops took the city of Lo-shan to the west and looted it. In the hope of destroying the society they also burned scores of villages. Society members from Hsin-hsien, Cheng-hsien, Ju-hsien, and other *hsien* united to attack Lo-shan and expel the Kiangsi troops. Thousands of society members attacked the city, their weapons like a forest of flags and spears, but they dispersed before taking it.[19] In April 1927 the Eighth Army of the Feng-tien forces, which had been running riot in a section of Lo-shan hsien, was attacked by the Red Spears and completely destroyed.[20]

In January 1927 Li Wan-ju, commander of the Tenth Division of the Chen-kao Army [Chen-kao-chün], was occupying the county seat of Hsi-nan. His troops were stationed in all the surrounding towns, where they forcibly collected taxes and were often unruly. To oppose them, some people in the eastern section of the *hsien* decided to organize a militia. They wished to imitate the Red Spears and affiliated themselves with the society's unit in Lo-yang. The troops of Chang Chih-kung were stationed in Lo-yang at the time and were in conflict with the Lo-yang Red Spears. They had killed the Red Spears leader, Wang Lien-san, and fighting was on the increase.

Chang ordered units of the Tenth Division stationed in Hsi-nan to come to the aid of Lo-yang. The Red Spears attacked the advancing troops. The fight lasted half a month, with the military commander, Li Wan-ju, unable to win a victory. Finally Li called on Ho Meng-keng, whose division was stationed in Shensi, and together the two commanders pillaged an area of several square miles, destroying over five thousand houses.[21]

In the spring of 1927 in the town of Ta-ming, Hsieh Yü-t'ien, commander of the First Army of the combined Chihli-Shantung forces, killed Liu Hsi-hsien, the well-known leader of the southern unit of the Red Spears. A battle commenced between the Red Spears and Hsieh's troops in Fei-hsien, Kuang-p'ing, and Ch'eng-an, and in Lin-chang hsien in Honan. After several days of heavy fighting, in which the city of Ta-ming changed hands several times, a joint military-civilian commission was established to negotiate a peace. This incident, too, is recorded in the gazetteer for Ta-ming hsien.[22]

One result of these many actions against warlord troops was that the KMT armies, marching northward on the Northern Expedition, also were attacked by society members.[23] In the autumn of 1927, after the KMT expeditionary forces reached An-yang, they were attacked by several secret societies and pushed south. The KMT brigade commander, Chi Hung-ch'ang, led his units against the villages controlled by the secret societies. Arriving in An-yang on 3 August 1927, he took the city, arrested many male citizens, and placed restrictions on several city organizations. Over a thousand people were killed.[24]

In September 1927 the Big Sword Society in Chiao-tung began a protest against warlord troops. When fighting ensued the provincial commissioner [*tu-pan*] Chang ordered his subordinate, Chu Hsiang, to handle the situation. Clashes between the Big Swords and the warlord troops occurred at Wang-t'ai between 3 and 8 September. The Big Swords suffered several hundred killed and several hundred weapons captured. Clashes between troops and secret societies such as the Big Swords or the United Village Society recurred intermittently in Chiao-tung until 1930.[25]

Section 3: Attacking Cities and Local Government

As the Red Spears grew, its organization became more complex. In addition to tax protests and actions against warlord troops, Red Spears units began attacking cities and local government officials. For example, in the autumn of 1923 the Red Spears attacked a government office in Shantung's Lin-chü hsien. They freed prisoners, burned some of the offices, and killed several local officials including the jailer, the recorder, and the chief of police.[26]

Another example is recorded, this one from Honan province. In 1923 Chao Shu-hsün (commander of the First Mixed Regiment surbordinated to the Shensi First Mixed Brigade, commanded by Kao Chün) and the Second Route Guards (commanded by Kuo Chin-pang) were stationed in Lu-shih hsien, Honan. Occasionally the two units would descend upon the *hsien* government officer, demanding pay. Chao's units required fourteen thousand *yüan* per month, in addition to food and incidentals, while Kuo's forces required fifteen thousand *yüan* per month, plus food and incidentals. The money was to be collected from the residents of the *hsien*.

The harvest was poor that year and by autumn the people realized that they could not furnish the necessary funds. In August societies such as the Red Spears, the Hard Stomach Corps [Ying-tu-tuei], the Crop Protection Society [Shou-wang she], and the self-defense corps mobilized several thousand members and surrounded the county seat. The *hsien* officials sent urgent reports to their superiors. The highest provincial officer, Ting Hsiang-ling, and a divisional commander named Han Yü-k'un each dispatched a special commander to investigate. As a result of negotiations with the rebels, the officials agreed to meet three conditions:

1. All of Kuo Chin-pang's troops would be withdrawn from the *hsien*.
2. The wages of Chao's forces would be reduced by half, with a monthly payment of seven thouand *yüan*; other provisions would also be halved.
3. Unauthorized military units would no longer be free to randomly seize people in the countryside.

In February 1924 several societies surrounded the city for a second time. When it was surrounded for a third time, in April, over one hundred thousand society members were involved.[27]

Often the Red Spears proved to be skilled negotiators, winning the admiration of the people. In June 1924 there was an uprising of the Big Sword Society of Liu-an in Anhwei. On 30 June they entered the county seat, proclaiming themselves the Army of the Society for Economic Improvement and Self-Government [Min-sheng ch'iu-chi tzu-chih hui chün]. They did not rob the merchants, but conferred with three British and American priests and the director of the chamber of commerce, asking that troops not be called in against them. They boasted, "Make it known publicly that our great military might is enough to make our enemies destroy themselves, since they would not know which way to turn." Then over three thousand society members attacked Ying-shan, Ho-fei, and other *hsien*. On 18 July they found themselves surrounded by warlord troops. Knowing their strength was insufficient to defeat these forces, they took twenty-five thousand *yüan* that had been donated by the chamber of commerce and retreated from Liu-an.[28]

Once a city was taken, some highly organized Red Spears units were actually capable of administering it. In February 1927 the county seat of Ch'üeh-shan, in Honan, was attacked by several Red Spears groups. The Fifth Eastern Unit [Tung-wu-pao] of the Red Spears was led by Chang Li-shan, the Sixth Eastern Units was led by Ou-yang Ping-yen, and the Northern Fifth Unit was led by Ma Hsiang-te. Together they attacked Ch'üeh-shan, where the Eighth Army, commanded by the warlord Li Jung-heng, had only a few weak units. The attack was launched on 3 March and the city occupied on 7 March.

Some looting occurred and the county magistrate, Wang Hsiao-ch'ü, was handcuffed and taken to jail. Occupying the offices of the county government, the Red Spears established a seven-man commission composed of Chang Li-shan, Chang Yao-ch'ang, Wang

Tse-hsien, Tung Tzu-hsiang, Li Jun-p'u, Chang Chia-to, and Ma
Hsiang-te, which ruled the county for three months. They divided
their troops into two large units, one commanded by Hsü Yao-ts'ai
and the other by Ou-yang Ping-yen. The county magistrate was
ransomed for two thousand *yüan.* [Despite their administrative
abilities] the Red Spears forces engaged in murder and other criminal
acts and soon won the enmity of the people. On 6 June 1927 over
one thousand people rose up against the society, forcing Chang
Li-shan and the others to flee the city by night.[29] This is one case in
which the Red Spears was not able to gain the loyalty of the local
inhabitants.

In some locations, the Red Spears united with other secret
societies to occupy and administer a city. On 3 March 1927 there
was an uprising of Red Spears in Ch'eng-an hsien, Hopei province. It
began when a branch of the self-defense militia in the village of
Kuo-san-ts'un distributed weapons to the people. On 19 March this
unit led the way in taking the county seat. Three societies, the Red
Spears, the Yellow Pebbles [Huang-sha], and the Heavenly Gate
Society established a joint headquarters within the city walls. They
handled all government affairs, including civil cases of debt, [criminal
cases of] assault and battery, and even cases of murder or injury.
The regular *hsien* officials did not interfere with the secret societies.
This state of affairs continued for several months.[30]

Red Spears members were always ready to take revenge
against authorities who caused deaths in their ranks. In June 1927
the county magistrate of An-lu hsien in Hupei, Sun Hsiang-ch'i, sent
a telegram to the Military Affairs Commission of the KMT at
Wuhan, explaining why a unit of Red Spears had attacked his county
seat. He said, "The uprising was caused by the fact that the KMT
party branch of An-lu executed two Red Spears leaders and the
Agricultural Cooperative Society killed six gentry who also happened
to be members of the organization. This caused a good deal of public
indignation among members of the Red Spears."[31]

Section 4: Robbing and Killing

The Red Spears gradually increased in number during the
twentieth century, until its membership was quite large. As it grew,
it came to include both good and bad elements and certain groups
began stealing from the people, cheating them, and forcing some,
including bandits, to join the society.[32] As bandits joined the Red

Spears in increasing numbers, acts of violence and pillage increased. The society came to be known as the Red Spears bandits.[33] This society, founded to protect the people, changed into a group that harassed them. In many localities the Red Spears began attacking cities, where its members wildly looted and killed.[34] Greatly alarmed, local governments began to reorganize militia units composed of Red Spears or other secret-society members, but the new groups were no more subject to legal authority than they had been before reorganization. For example, in December 1926 the Red Spears Society in Hsin-ho hsien in Hopei, headed by Wang Tung-ch'eng and Chao Chun-ling, was subdivided into two guard regiments. The units were stationed in the county seat and were supposed to receive their pay and provisions from the local residents. During the day society members patrolled the nearby villages, often demanding food and money. At night they took their spears and engaged in violent acts against the people. The gentry and villagers were at a loss as to how they could solve this problem, so they wrote congratulatory banners, calling the society the "Protectors of Ten Thousand People," and describing it as "Loved and Supported by Ten Thousand People." But such flattery did not lessen the illegal actions of the members.

On 9 January 1928 the Red Spears stationed in the Hsin-ho county seat began marching through the eastern section of the old city demanding money. They clashed with the local militia. The Red Spears suffered many wounded and killed and its units were scattered. That evening the society forces fled the city.[35]

In 1927 in southern Hopei, a man named Chang, who was the leader of the Red Spears, was given a medal by the local government and his society was converted to an army brigade, of which he was made commander. His unit was stationed in Nan-kung City, but illegal activities by the members of his group, including extortion, continued. This was reported to the county magistrate, Wang Shou-hsien, who ordered Chang arrested and held at the offices of the *hsien* government. The defense commissioner in the area was asked to advise the local government on what to do. He disbanded the local branch of the Red Spears and had Chang shot. However, the Red Spears in Nan-kung rose again in 1928 and, with a membership of three or four thousand, attacked residents in the countryside surrounding the city. Many people were killed, including Wang Ching-jen, the chief of police. Resistance to the rampaging units was offered by local self-defense forces, who killed many Red Spears members.[36]

There are other examples of fights between secret societies. For example, in 1927 more than two hundred members of the Heavenly Gate Society of Yung-nien hsien in Hopei attacked the county seat of nearby Nan-ho hsien. The county magistrate was taken prisoner and over two thousand *yüan* removed from the treasury. More than two thousand members of the Red Spears Society in Yung-nien hsien surrounded the county seat and battled with the Heavenly Gate Society throughout the night. The Heavenly Gate Society was no match for the Red Spears, who entered the city and killed more than seventy Heavenly Gate members.[37]

There are more examples of fighting between the Red Spears and other secret societies. When conflicts arose, the boundaries of the societies' territories were carefully marked and jealously defended. Intrusion into the territory of another society was the cause of many deaths.[38]

Section 5: Opposing Conscription

The practice of raising armies has been common throughout China's long history. In general, most of the soldiers recruited for such armies were vagabonds, petty thieves, or the very poor. Most joined the armies in desperation, simply to keep body and soul together.[39] These conditions came to be associated with military service in the popular mind, as reflected in the saying, "Good iron is not used to make nails and good men do not become soldiers."[40]

In the early years of the Republic, when warlord skirmishes continuously occurred, many warlords recruited vagabonds and even bandits to increase their personal power. When these elements threatened rebellion, the government would dispatch an official to negotiate their demands, and this was called "pacification."[41] Because the warlord armies were composed of many diverse elements, rape, arson, and looting were common. The people grew to fear and hate the warlord troops. Only later, during the war against Japan, were regular recruitment systems established in China to supplement conscription. Although many people now view military service as a precious right, or even a sacred responsibility, the traditional Chinese attitude was that "Good men do not become soldiers; those who are soldiers are not good men." Few could comprehend the concept of "serving with glory" and many deserted the army.

Sons from wealthy families who wished to avoid the rigors of military service or were disinclined to sacrifice themselves for a warlord, paid high prices to secure a substitute to serve in their place. This system was known as "having someone to take your place" [man-ming ting-t'i].[42] It was possible to do this under the Republic, because there was no standard system of identification and photographs were not in use. To earn money, it was a common practice to enter a military unit under a false name, then desert and reenter another unit under a second false name. Such persons were called "people who would sell themselves to the army" [mai-cheng-ping].

The various military districts were guarded,[43] and to prevent new soldiers from deserting, recruits often were bound together in groups of three or five and were marched, like convicts, with armed guards on either side. I witnessed such sights during the Republican period. As for barracks, the troops usually were billeted in small temples or schools. In winter they lacked blankets and in summer they were not given mosquito nets. Often they slept on the floor. Infectious insects abounded and human filth littered their quarters. (At that time the ever-present lice were called "anti-Japanese bugs.") They could not keep themselves clean, could not change clothes, and the sick did not receive medical attention. Recruits rarely ate well because, although the government authorized at least twenty-one ounces of white rice per soldier per day, in addition to sufficient vegatables, unscrupulous officers and NCOs often kept two-thirds of the rations for their own use. Besides slowly sapping the strength of each man in this manner, officers often shaved the heads of recruits so it would be easy to identify them if they escaped. Of course, the officers enjoyed meat, fish, and rice wine.

Many recruits brought money or clothing with them, but these were usually confiscated to make desertion impossible. When a recruit died, the government authorized provision of a coffin and fees for a burial, but the money usually went to middlemen and often only a burial shroud was supplied. There were many deserters from the warlord armies. When someone escaped, others would be conscripted. This continual round of escapes and conscriptions existed alongside the practice of "selling oneself to the army."

Those who were not drafted saw the situation growing worse and worse and knew that the newly conscripted soldiers were treated as prisoners and animals.[44] Therefore, many young men would hide in the surrounding hills and fields by day, often near starvation, and at night would try to find their way home. Some of those who avoided conscription in Kwangtung or Fukien provinces eventually landed in Singapore.[45] When recruiting officers needed men, they would order their troops to enter villages at night, surround the houses, and forcibly take the young men. This practice is recalled in a book, which states,

> The *pao-chia* chief in every *hsien* assisted the local army commander by inspecting all the houses in a village every evening. When young sons of suitable or unsuitable age were found at home they were siezed by the *pao-chia* chief. Many families were poor and if there was only one son his mother and wife would weep and wail.
>
> One time we captured some travelling peddlers, who pleaded for release, but we could not let them go. As we travelled along we said nothing. This sort of thing occurs elsewhere, but it is worst in Honan.
>
> Whenever we gathered a number of recruits, we were afraid they might escape, so sometimes we kept them in a guarded room like convicts. Sometimes we tied them; they were treated worse than convicts. Who would not fear this situation, and what son of a rich family would wish to become a soldier? Nothing can be said to justify such a system. Many people grieve over it, but still it persists.[46]

The situation reached the point where young men were captured in broad daylight and, with their heads shaved, were marched off to become soldiers. This caused much bitterness among the peasants and it prompted the Red Spears to begin opposing conscription.

In the spring of 1943 the Red Spears (locally called the Big Sword Society) was very active in the area of Ning-te, Lo-yüan, Fu-an, and nearby *hsien* in Fukien province. Many peasants who joined the society to avoid the army began anticonscription activities. On one occasion the Thirty-third Brigade of the government's Third Military Command Region, stationed in the western section of Ning-te hsien, was ordered to curtail Red Spears activities. The brigade commander, Tseng Kua, ordered the 698th Regiment, commanded by Chang Mo-ching, into the field. Chang assembled several columns of troops and left Ning-te, marching southeast.

The Red Spears forces in the vicinity were divided into large, medium, and small units, each composed of several hundred men. They wore ordinary clothing, except for a red scarf tied around their heads, which served as a means of identification. When they assembled in the hills or fields, gathering before their leader, he would first pray to the gods, then give instructions to the men. Then the members would drink a magic potion, grasp their red-tasseled spears, and depart. The leader carried a flag with seven stars.[47] According to regulations, the men were to travel in two columns, to the right and left of the leader, but on occasion they marched in no special formation.

Walking at the front of his column, the leader donned a red monk's robe and wore a copper band on his head, wider in the front than in the back.[48] The leader also was distinguished by a steel ring, attached to a brass stick and carried in the left hand, which made a sound when shaken, and by his trumpet, usually a conch shell, carried in the right hand.

The Red Spears attacked the government troops, arrayed on a mountaintop. The government forces had many kinds of guns, which they fired at the Red Spears. But, even though many members were killed, the survivors continued advancing and could not be stopped. The Red Spears leader ordered his men not to look back or turn and run, because this would render the magic potion ineffective and bullets would pierce their bodies. The leader stood atop the mountain, blowing upon his trumpet and shaking his brass stick faster and faster. Responding to his call, the Red Spears attacked more savagely. Many local men were in the government ranks and they knew the superstition that Red Spears members could not be killed. As they saw the Red Spears coming closer and closer, their belief was reinforced and they became very frightened. Although the Red Spears suffered many casualties, they eventually overcame the government troops, which were forced to retreat.

The officers of the government forces knew that the charms and potions of the Red Spears were ineffective, but they also knew that their troops believed in ghosts and spirits and were frightened by the idea of magic charms used against them. So the government officers changed their strategy to one that would avoid open confrontation. They began to hide behind the walls of peasant compounds and throw grenades at Red Spears members as they passed the front gates. They also planned a sort of psychological warfare in which superstition would combat superstition. Many of their troops were local residents who believed that the blood of a dog could negate magic charms and increase strength. Before engaging in battle with the Red Spears, the government officers would have several dogs killed and their blood smeared on the troop's bullets, artillery shells, and hand grenades, telling their men that now the Red Spears charms would be useless and they could kill the society members without fear. The troops believed their leaders and their courage increased. The Red Spears forces, learning that the government troops had found a way to overcome their magic charms, grew frightened and within two months were defeated.

In conclusion, let me say that the transformation of the Red Spears into an organization that engaged in criminal activities had many causes, most of them unrelated to the nature of the society and its members. Rather, the society's goal of self-protection prompted its members to engage in tax protests, to oppose military conscription, and so on. One could say that their behavior was the natural reaction of "an exhausted and powerless people scattered before forces they did not understand."[49]

Chapter VII: Accomplishments of the Red Spears

Section 1: The Soviet Communists and the Red Spears

The involvement of the Soviet communists with the Red Spears Society began with a report by a man named Solovyeff who was attached to the Soviet embassy in Peking. He reported that he considered the Red Spears the first manifestation of a strong revolutionary peasant movement. This conclusion was echoed in the Eleventh Resolution Concerning the China Problem, adopted at the Seventh Session of the Third Comintern, which read,

> Concerning China and other areas, the responsibility of the Communist Party is to encourage struggles against the feudal system, warlordism, and imperialism among those who are under the control of reactionaries. This is the best method for crushing antirevolutionary armies. The Communist Party should use various peasant groups, such as the Red Spears, and should try to join their organizations."[1]

In carrying out this resolution, the Soviet communists ordered some of their members to join the Red Spears and to begin using the society for their own ends. The activities of these members did in fact strengthen the Red Spears militarily. Under the influence of the Soviet communists, a Provincial Peasants Assembly was organized in April 1925, though of the fourteen or fifteen people who attended were all members of the Communist Party. This probably reflects the fact that in the early stages of their work with the peasants the communists were unable to involve the masses.

The Soviet communists continued their efforts to create an armed self-defense corps and of the thirteen persons who attended their second meeting, only six were Communist Party members; the remainder were Red Spears leaders. Of the officers elected at that meeting, three were Communist Party members and six were Red

Spears leaders. In addition, the Communist Party dispatched political and military advisors to help the Red Spears. Although neither of these advisors were particularly successful in influencing the Red Spears units, when the Feng-tien armies of Chang Tso-lin were attacking Honan, they acknowledged that the Red Spears preserved themselves by maintaining neutrality and not opposing the warlord armies.

Soviet communists sent to Honan to work with the Red Spears reported on other party members who were doing the same: "Yao Pin-shuang is with the Red Spears at T'a-ho, Huang Wen-ch'ing is with the Red Spears at Lo-yang, and Comrade Ying is with the Red Spears in Wei-hsien, while Comrade Tai is working with the Red Spears in the district of Yen."[2]

One Red Spears leader, Sun Hun-you, was very powerful in eastern Honan, southern Shantung, and northern Anhwei. The Soviets dispatched Hu Tse-li to assist Sun with his activities in the south. Sun agreed that Hu should undertake various actions in the southern part of his territory and Hu took responsibility for matters concerning money and military supplies. Later a split occurred because Hu embezzled funds allocated to finance the movement in the south.

Despite such occurrences, the Soviets sometimes succeeded in using the Red Spears to their own advantage. For example, the Hsü-ch'ang Red Spears' unit, which included forty thousand men and ten thousand carbines, all the leaders joined the Communist Party and followed the directives of the Soviets. Under Soviet leadership the Hsü-ch'ang Red Spears gained two victories over Chang Tso-lin's armies and withheld taxes in Ch'ang-ko hsien and Lin-ying hsien. About the same time a leader of the Society of the Mysterious Way, Chang Ching-hsiu, in western Honan, was very close to the Soviet communists. Chang's willingness to cooperate was attributed by the communists to the fact that "we have already bribed him." Later, when funds diminished, "Chang sold himself to another warlord."

Because of such incidents, the Soviets usually were unsuccessful in courting the Red Spears. The Soviets' distain is evident in their "Report Concerning the Red Spears in Honan and the Work of Party Members," which stated,

1. We have thirty-five party members working with the Red Spears.
2. Twelve areas are represented by these members.

3. The Red Spears has fifty thousand members in urban areas such as Chi-nan, Hsü-ch'ang, and Lo-yang, and in provinces such as Honan, Anhwei, Kiangsu, and southern Shantung.

4. On 17 September we held a meeting and decided to order the establishment of party organizations and a Worker's Central Bureau. Enthusiastic reports were delivered by all the representatives at the meeting, recommending that the Worker's Central Bureau in each locality join forces with local Red Spears to form a united organization.

Unfortunately, the districts represented at this meeting were too few to begin a successful movement. Most of the representatives were comrades we had sent to work with the Red Spears. Because of this we anticipate some difficulty in forming united organizations.[3]

At that time the Red Spears had at least three million members in Honan, Shantung, Kiangsu, southern Hopei, and northern Anhwei, but the communists had only thirty-five people representing twelve areas, possibly working with only fifty thousand Red Spears members. Most of the communists were party members dispatched by the Soviets; only a few were Red Spears leaders. Thus, Soviet efforts to influence Chinese political and military life had no real impact. This is demonstrated in a "Report on the Red Spears in Honan Aiding the Northern Expedition." The report details the destruction of rail lines and Red Spears units under communist direction. The intent was to prevent the use of railroads by warlord troops and harassment of the forces of Wu P'ei-fu. The report admits that these activities were thinly spread and that the Red Spears also suffered losses.[4]

It is clear from the report that the Soviet communist attempts to alter the political situation in China were insufficient, often amounting to nothing more than propaganda. There is also some doubt as to the effectiveness of the attempts to destroy rail and telegraph lines and to mobilize peasants to oppose Wu P'ei-fu. It is absurd to think that the two or three thousand rubles spent by the Soviet communists were sufficient to organize the Red Spears as a popular self-defense group. Twenty or thirty thousand rubles would not have been enough to control the Red Spears throughout Honan. Those who were bought were only a small percentage of the membership, often undisciplined or not trusted by the rest of the group. Such people had little influence. In the end the Soviets were unsuccessful in their attempts to use the Red Spears.

Section 2: The Chinese Communists and the Red Spears

Since the Chinese Communist Party was interested in organizing the peasant movement, it decided to infiltrate the leadership of the Red Spears whenever possible. In June 1926 Ch'en Tu-hsiu published an article in the *Hsiang-tao Weekly* entitled "The Red Spears and Chinese Peasant Uprisings," which included the statement, "The Red Spears, who are supported by the great masses of the peasants, are active in Honan, Shantung, and the southern part of Chihli, in Anhwei, Kiangsu, and the northern part of Kiangsi. Can we let the movement run its own course, or should we lead them under the banner of antiimperialism and antiwarlordism? This is an important question facing China today."[5]

Li Ta-chao published an article entitled "The Red Spears in Shantung, Honan, and Shensi," taking as his theme the defeat by the Red Spears in Honan of the Second Kuo-min Army warlord Feng Yü-hsiang and concluding that the strength of the peasant class was indeed sufficient to defeat warlordism. Of the peasant victories he said, "These victories document the strength of the peasant classes, which can triumph over warlordism and crush the renegade units. The victories also prove that these same peasants can protect their class and destroy all warlord armies. They can rise above their own class interests and hasten the fate of warlordism, which will be destroyed."[6]

Li recognized that an armed peasant movement could not only oppose the warlords, but would encourage peasants in warlord armies to desert, thereby increasing the number of able-bodied men in the villages, the bases from which warlord power would be destroyed.[7] But, Li continued, in assuming the leadership of the Red Spears, some of the society's basic precepts would have to be dealt with. These included antiforeignism, worship of the Buddha, and superstitious beliefs, all contrary to the principles of the Communist Party.

In order to assume leadership of the Red Spears, Li Ta-chao proposed that "We should guide the Red Spears to a correct understanding of the nature of imperialism and turn some of their anger toward those who are oppressing China. We must change their narrow-minded, racist views and teach them to understand that revolutionary workers and peasants throughout the world are their friends."

Li regarded the Red Spears' worship of Buddha as the expession of a typical peasant desire for political stability. He wrote, "We must tell them that the only means of achieving peace is through the unity of the workers and peasants." About superstitious practices he wrote, "When the peasants have guns and cannon, they will no longer use magic charms. When modern weapons are in their hands, superstitions concerning the five elements and eight trigrams will lose their effectiveness."[8]

The Chinese Communist Party was particularly interested in the concept of class, which led Li to write, "We must make typical peasants understand their class relationship in order to change their provincial outlook to a class outlook. . . . We should urge them to organize and unite." Li felt that the use of the Red Spears by warlords was "a practice which directly threatens to crush armed peasant organizations" and "must be guarded against." Since both arms and men had become commodities used by the warlords and gentry, Li concluded "Our slogan should call for armed, peasant, self-defense organizations to be established in villages, with as many members as possible to ensure mutual protection and aid." He urged young people, rural primary-school teachers, intelligentsia, and peasant activists to quickly enroll in the Red Spears and then transform the society into an armed self-defense group.[9]

Because of their interest in the Red Spears, the second enlarged meeting of the Central Committee of the Chinese Communist Party passed a resolution, which stated,

> 1. The Red Spears Society is a product of warlord politics. Its members are the typical middle and small peasants who cannot bear the extortion of corrupt officials, the multitude of unfair taxes, the destruction caused by warfare, and the vexations of bandits and renegade soldiers. They bear the havoc wreaked by inflation in the imperialist economy and they are treated no better than the fish and meat of the wealthy landlords. The Red Spears began as a peasant organization, but later various unwholesome

elements joined or the leadership of the society fell into the hands of rich gentry. Still, it cannot be said that the Red Spears is a bandit organization. . . .

2. Not only is the Red Spears one of the most important forces in the national revolutionary movement, but it helps promote the important aim, which all must recognize, of peasant cooperation. . . .

3. The Red Spears is a significant force in the mass opposition to warlord politics, but it must unite with other revolutionary groups to break down its defeatist elements and counterrevolutionary naiveté. Because of its desultory organization and superstitions it is not always effective in battle and it displays tendencies toward destructiveness and disunity.

4. We should give the Red Spears an organizational method and a policy of action. These should be very simple and easy to understand. As to organizational method, the first step should be to urge local groups to unite with other Red Spears units to form a secret communications network, so that each warn others of danger and provide assistance. This communications base could be initiated by our comrades in the Red Spears, first as an intelligence-gathering unit and later as a leadership unit. After the communications network is established, the second step should be to call a meeting of leaders of the Red Spears, Black Spears, and other secret societies in order to establish a simple organization and a single plan of action. This plan must include the following points: (a) oppose bandits; (b) oppose the depredations of undisciplined military units; (c) oppose miscellaneous surtaxes; (d) oppose military conscription; (e) oppose the circulation of military script; (f) protect local stability (by participating in local self-government work); (g) ensure that local finances are kept honest and ethical; and (h) oppose corrupt officials. These

slogans must be phrased in simple language, which peasants can easily understand. If the Red Spears act under these slogans, they will be genuine self-defense organizations and can seek to participate in self-government, but we must not let these groups attain political power.

5. We must not oppose the superstitious beliefs of the Red Spears. They are the basis upon which the society organizes and struggles. While they are merely the trappings of a concept the peasants cannot abandon, we should make sure these superstitious activities ultimately benefit the revolution.

6. Under the special conditions that exist in Honan and Shantung, we should encourage the true peasant Red Spears to unite with the bandit-infiltrated Red Spears and those in the employ of rich gentry, because they all oppose Chang Tsung-ch'ang and Wu P'ei-fu. We must encourage them to form a united front in opposition to warlord governments and at the same time reinforce the true peasant organizations.

7. The leadership of the Red Spears often falls into the hands of the rich landlords. Also, the bandit-infiltrated Red Spears assist the landlords and they are very effective in battle. If it happens that we cannot unite the Red Spears groups under the banner of opposition to warlord government, our next step should be to ensure that the true peasant Red Spears are not influenced by the bandit factions. Then we must see that the bandit-infiltrated Red Spears are not used by anyone else; we must try to persuade the "bandit" groups to stand with the peasants in opposition to the landlords."[10]

In March 1927 a report sent from Honan to the Central Committee in Wuhan stated, "The Red Spears exists in every *hsien* of Honan. It has over one million members, of which our party could only lead two to three hundred thousand. It is very difficult for our comrades when Red Spears members slip from our influence and revert to their old beliefs. If we want to have influence in Honan, we must send funds to help our comrades in the peasant movement there."[11] About the same time the local party, hoping to increase its membership in Honan, held a Meeting of Representatives of the Honan Armed Peasants [Honan wu-chuang nung-min tai-piao tu-hui].[12]

The Central Committee also wished to strengthen the peasant movement in Honan, so it organized a War Zone Peasant Movement Committee [Chan-ch'u nung-min yün-tung wei-yüan-hui] and dispatched forty students from the Peasant Movement Institute to Honan.[13] Teng Liang-sheng, the peasant movement cadre who was sent by the Central Committee to Honan, reported,

> Previously we were not too concerned with Honan. We did not understand the situation there and had not settled upon a work plan. Reports from many areas say that Honan peasants are very revolutionary. Now we are turning our attention to Honan in preparation for leading the peasants in revolutionary work and our hopes are very high. We were very disappointed upon our arrival to discover that conditions in society and among the peasants were not as they had been reported. We found we were facing great difficulties in our work.
>
> When we were in Kuang-shui we observed the local Red Spears, who were just beginning to destroy rail lines. At that time our comrades, along with our troops, approached the village reactionaries and explained to the Red Spears the importance of the current Northern Expedition. When our special agents went to work in various localities, they traveled with the troops; if they did not do so, they found themselves in great danger. This was a most difficult situation. Later, when we arrived in Chu-ma-tien, we held a special meeting. In addition to the comrades who had been dispatched there already, participants included representatives from the provincial party committees and comrades from the General Political Council [Tsung cheng-chih-pu]. We adopted a propaganda plan for Honan, which called for dispatching comrades to various localities.

First we sent comrades to the areas where we had political connections. Because the Honan peasants are very old-fashioned and conservative, having predominantly feudal attitudes, our propaganda work was very difficult and we could not use our standard slogans and phrases. We were forced to change our tactics and distribute propaganda in official-looking documents, with a seal affixed, in order to effectively communicate our ideas to the people.

We have encountered other difficulties, some involving the Red Spears Society, which is not a true revolutionary group, but the sort of feudal organization that obeys the commands of the landlords. Our revolutionary work in the peasant villages called for persuading the people to strike down the landlords, while the Red Spears supports them. This is a most difficult problem. Furthermore, their thinking is very backward and they accept the blandishments of the reactionaries who claim, among other things, that the KMT favors prostitution.

On one occasion, when Red Spears members saw a poster concerning the League of Peasants, Workers, Businessmen, Students, Soldiers, and Women, which had been issued by the Central Political Bureau, they said it was proof of prostitution. Because they are like children, they are very easily influenced by reactionary propaganda, with the result that they will not support the KMT and the National Revolutionary Army. This also poses great difficulties for us. We have very few responsible comrades to do our work and they have little experience. Most of the comrades dispatched here are from southern Honan and because of the differences in dialects are not easily understood in the north. We encounter many problems of this sort.

At present about 80 percent of the local inhabitants cultivate their own land, but because the crop yields are low even peasants who have several score *mou* cannot support themselves. Of course, they cannot employ helpers. Among the peasants near Lo-yang are many who barely survive and, because their lives are so difficult, it is almost impossible for them to participate in revolutionary work."[14]

The phrase, "they will not support the KMT and the National Revolutionary Army," did not refer to the KMT proper, but to the forces that were then composed of the KMT and Chinese Communist Party members. Although the Red Spears in Honan did not always support the KMT, society announcements who that there was some respect for Sun Yat-sen and his Three Principles of the People.[15]

Trouble often erupted between the Red Spears and the KMT armies of the Northern Expedition. For example, a clash occurred in Hsin-yang, Honan, between society members and comrades working in the peasant movement at the beginning of May 1927. When the local party branch decided to execute twenty-four prominent gentry, the Red Spears mobilized in their defense. Communist propaganda workers claimed that reactionary power was so strong in the area that peasants were afraid to join the KMT-CCP-sponsored Peasant's Association. Over a thousand Red Spears members attacked the KMT-CCP party cadres, killing fifteen and capturing one, whom they attempted to execute but finally released. A report on the incident concluded, "Hsin-yang is completely controlled by reactionaries and it is very difficult to carry out our work."[16]

Occasionally the KMT reacted by ordering its members to refrain from provoking the peasants.[17] Despite this, clashes contined to occur in Hupei province as well as in Honan. An especially large uprising of Red Spears members against KMT personnel in Hupei was reported by Teng Yen-ta in a speech given on 24 June 1927. At least five major clashes occurred between troops of the Northern Expedition and the Red Spears in Hupei, in June and July 1927. As a result, the peasant movement was never fully developed in Hupei.

Section 3: Impact of the Red Spears

Because of their commitment to protecting the peasants from bandits and renegade soldiers, the Red Spears had a great impact on the countryside. Its effectiveness was such that banditry was controlled and the excesses of renegade warlord troops were kept in check. The society was actually a major force in preserving local stability. Although several Red Spears units turned to banditry and caused damage in some areas, the instances of illegal acts were in fact quite few. The majority of the Red Spears members maintained good relations with other peasants and sincerely wished to help them, without consideration of political ideologies.

The Red Spears became especially strong in north China and after they helped defeat various warlord armies, many government officials acknowledged their power. For example, the Red Spears assisted Wu P'ei-fu in defeating the Second Kuo-min Army of Feng Yü-hsiang. After Wu was driven from Lo-yang, the Second Kuo-min Army, commanded by Hu Ching-i, entered Honan in December 1924. When Hu died in April 1925, Yüeh Wei-chün assumed leadership and the army underwent a thorough reorganization.[18] With this army and other units stationed in the province, Honan had at least two hundred thousand troops within its borders. To maintain these forces, at least two million *yüan* were required for expenses and supplies. The falling value of the local currency and the increasing need to raise money for the troops resulted in numerous taxes and surtaxes imposed upon the people. Wu P'ei-fu dispatched agents to the local Red Spears and told them that if Yüeh's Kuo-min troops were driven out, Wu would cancel taxes for three years and abolish surtaxes.[19]

In response to these promises, more than one million Red Spears members assisted Wu in driving the Kuo-min armies from the province. Red Spears units blocked the route of the retreating Kuo-min Army in January 1926 and continued their attacks in the following month, defeating two hundred thousand of Yüeh's troops within ten days.[20] In addition, another thirty or forty thousand men and more than one hundred railroad cars loaded with arms were destroyed.[21] Thus it can be said that the strength of the Red Spears helped Wu P'ei-fu defeat the Second Kuo-min Army of Yüeh Wei-chün.

The Red Spears also assisted the KMT National Revolutionary Army in defeating Wu P'ei-fu and the Feng-tien Army. Of course, the society had originally helped Wu come to power in Honan, but the depredations of his troops brought about a change of attitude. In the beginning, after Yüeh's forces withdrew from Honan, the people welcomed Wu's armies and believed that their troubles were ended. How were they to know that, of Wu's two hundred thousand men, not many had rifles and even fewer had ammunition? How were they to know that the soldiers' uniforms were worn and ragged and that they would burden the people in order to reequip themselves? Taxes of all kinds and destructive behavior became the order of the day. A tax was placed on the number of rooms within a building, a special tax on kerosene was imposed, and the circulation of nonconvertible script of questionable value was enforced. Money was withdrawn from the provincial bank, trees were felled along the banks of the Yellow River, and even government land was sold to raise money for the troops.[22]

As more taxes were instituted in various *hsien*, the people began to see that Wu's promise to delay tax collection for three years and abolish surtaxes was valueless. Although some Red Spears leaders were appointed to positions within the provincial army, Wu soon claimed that the province was at peace and ordered these forces demobilized. The Red Spears came to detest Wu's troops even more than they had hated the Kuo-min Army and they resolved to drive Wu's forces from the province. When the KMT National Revolutionary Armies reached Honan in 1927, the Red Spears joined them in attacking Wu, forcing him to retreat to Szechuan. After the defeat of Wu P'ei-fu, several hundred Red Spears leaders held a meeting in K'ai-feng and organized a self-defense army for the province with themselves at its head.[23]

The National Revolutionary Armies received much assistance from both the Red Spears and the Heavenly Gate Society in attacks against the warlord armies of Chang Tso-lin. Due to Red Spears assistance between January and June of 1927, warlord armies were defeated and forced to retreat in Honan, Shantung, and Anhwei. Typical of this assistance was a case in May 1927 in which the Red Spears helped the KMT armies attack Lo-yang and captured over twenty thousand Feng-tien Army warlord troops. As the Feng-tien troops retreated eastward, Red Spears units throughout Honan harassed them at every point.[24]

Chapter VIII: Conclusion

The Red Spears originated in the early years of the Republic as a popularly supported self-defense organization, composed of people who could no longer bear the banditry and lawless acts of renegade warlord troops. Red Spears units were based in peasant villages and small towns and were led by village elders or gentry from the landlord class. Later the character of the society changed, as rich landlords and vagabonds joined in increasing numbers. The society was known by many names, but generally it retained the goal of protecting the people and providing mutual aid.

As banditry became rampant in the Republican period, the primary function of the organization became protection against these roving groups. Later many bandits joined warlord armies which in many ways became worse than the original bandit groups. Society members came to hate the warlord armies. As the warlords increased their taxes and other depredations against the people, the Red Spears turned to tax protests. But, regardless of whether they were opposing bandits and warlord troops or protesting excessive taxes, they maintained their initial goal of self-defense. Whenever any unit of the society faced strong enemies, it could count on help from other Red Spears forces.

Society members drew upon various superstitions to arouse their fighting spirit and maintain high morale. The belief that spirits entered into members' bodies making it impossible for bullets to kill them was widely accepted. It is commonly believed that superstitions are abandoned as a culture develops. China has a history of several thousand years of highly developed culture. Why, then, was superstition so firmly entrenched among its people in the twentieth century, the age of science? The answer lies in an understanding of China's traditional culture. More than a thousand years of belief in spirits and ghosts and the influence of religious Taoism fostered the idea that peasants could make themselves safe from bullets by magic.

A long line of Chinese emperors and kings used such superstitions to impress the common people with their own divinity.

115

In the official histories of China from the traditional period, the founder of a dynasty was often portrayed as a god rather than a man. If the founders themselves were not depicted as gods, they were represented as the sons of gods. Ancient emperors generally called themselves the "sons of heaven" [t'ien-tzu]. The logic behind this deception was that, since the son of heaven ruled everything under heaven, the common people must obey him unquestioningly; with power so great, none would be able to oppose him.

Moreover, shameless scholars emphasized the myth that it was improper to rebel and a high crime to kill a ruler, until this was accepted as the truth. The people were taught loyalty to the ruler rather than loyalty to the nation. Rulers used such devices as a means of extending their control. Changes in leadership were explained as expressions of the heavenly will rather than the works of mortal men and rulers always used such methods to establish their legitimacy. Confucian scholars took the political philosophy of a peaceful world belonging to the people and changed it to a philosophy in which "the world is mine and belongs to me." This egocentric imperial philosophy is expressed in such traditional Chinese sayings as "My Blessings Extend over the Four Seas" [chen-fu yu szu-hai].

Firmly established in the traditional period, such thinking was revived by the warlords during the early Republic. The concept of "the legitimate ruler" [chen-ming t'ien-tzu] was similar in many ways to "the divine right of kings." Although the Chinese concept of the legitimate ruler had a slightly different meaning during the Republic, the basic premise was the same and its acceptance is reflected in such phrases as "constitutional monarchy" which were in common use at the time. Although the government eventually tried to suppress superstituous practices and beliefs, thousand of years of tradition could not be changed overnight, especially in the villages where they were deeply rooted.

The influence of religious Taoism was another factor in the perpetuation of these beliefs. Taoism began during the Eastern Han (25-220 A.D.) and over the course of a thousand years became very popular among the common people. Its influence on Chinese culture was great and may be compared to the influence of Christianity on European society. Certainly, as late as 1931 most Chinese peasants had not abandoned their belief in Taoism. As in Taiwan today, people practiced Taoist fortune-telling and selected dates for important events such as weddings with the aid of Taoist formulae. Many current practices among the Chinese on Taiwan, such as asking a Taoist priest to select a grave site or hanging pictures of spirits to protect against calamity, are based on Taoist beliefs.

With such deeply ingrained and all-pervasive beliefs, it was inevitable that the Red Spears membership would believe in the efficacy of magic charms and secret signs. Probably the strongest and most widespread popular organization in China at the time, the Red Spears Society, was imbued with superstituous beliefs and practices.

The Chinese are often characterized as a people resigned to fate, who will suffer much hardship and still work patiently and will starve rather than turn to banditry. There are many examples of times of famine in Chinese history when people were reduced to eating the bark of trees. Despite the fact that thousands died, the people did not turn to brigandry. From such examples one might draw the conclusion that the Chinese are the most law-abiding people on earth. Even in the midst of a famine, most people retained the ingrained beliefs, fostered by centuries of emperors, that the legitimate ruler was an expression of heaven's will and that mere humans were incapable of affecting that will. As a result, the masses had no particular political viewpoint. They accepted the saying "whoever is on the emperor's throne, pay him taxes and rice" and did not concern themselves with the individual on the throne. Thus, it can be said that the Chinese are one of the easiest people in the world to rule.

After the founding of the Republic, civil wars became endemic throughout the nation. The political system collapsed and society itself was in turmoil. Banditry and robbery were widespread and it seemed that no single individual could save the situation. Officials neglected their duties and abandoned the countryside to warlord armies. It as under such conditions that the Red Spears arose as a self-defense organization. Initially it had no political basis, although its activities broadened as increasingly diverse elements joined its ranks. Some Red Spears members engaged in banditry and looting, which in those cases changed the society from an organization protecting the people to an organization harmful to the people.

In spite of occasional excesses, however, the large majority of Red Spears members remained committed to the goals of defending the people against bandits, upholding peace, opposing warlord armies, and in general protecting the nation and its people. In that capacity they had a great impact, especially during the war with

Japan when they resisted the invasion of the Japanese armies. They wrote a glorious history for themselves during that period and fully demonstrated the heroic spirit of the Chinese people.

Notes

The Red Spears Reconsidered, by Elizabeth J. Perry

1. Tai Hsüan-chih, *I-ho-t'uan yen-chiu* [Study of the Boxers] (Taipei: Chung-kuo hsüeh-shu chu-tso chiang-chu wei-yüan-hui, 1963).
2. For an extended discussion of these sources, see Elizabeth J. Perry, *Rebels and Revolutionaries in North China, 1845-1945* (Stanford: Stanford University Press, 1980), 284-85.
3. Susan Naquin, *Millenarian Rebellion in China: The Eight Trigrams Uprising of 1813* (New Haven: Yale University Press, 1976), 30-31.
4. Susan Naquin, *Shantung Rebellion: The Wang Lun Uprising of 1774* (New Haven: Yale University Press, 1981), 100.
5. See Philip A. Kuhn's review of Tai Hsüan-chih's book on the Boxers in *Journal of Asian Studies* 25, no. 4 (August 1966): 760-61.
6. See Perry, *Rebels and Revolutionaries*, 267.
7. Mitani Takashi, "Kokumin kakumei jiki no hoppō nōmin bōdō" [Northern peasant uprisings during the time of the national revolution], in *Chūgoku kokumin kakumeishi no kenkyū*, ed. Nozawa Yutaka (Tokyo: Aoki shoten, 1974), 273.
8. Baba Takeshi, "Kōsōkai" [Red Spears], *Shakai Keizaishi Gaku*, 42, no. 1 (1976): 59-83.
9. Mitani Takashi, "Dentōteki nōmin tōsō no shintenkai" [New developments in traditional peasant struggles], in *Kōza Chūgoku kingendaishi* vol. 5, ed. Nozawa Yutaka and Tanaka Masatoshi (Tokyo: Tokyo University Press, 1978), 144.
10. Mitani, "Kokumin kakumei jiki no hoppō nōmin bōdō," 273; Perry, *Rebels and Revolutionaries*, 195-97.
11. Baba, "Kōsōkai," 60.
12. Baba Takeshi, "Kōsōkai undō josetsu" [Introduction to the Red Spears], in *Chūgoku minshu hanran no sekai* (Tokyo: Namiyoshi shoten, 1974), 143.

13. Ralph Thaxton, *China Turned Rightside Up: Revolutionary Legitimacy in the Peasant World* (New Haven: Yale University Press, 1983), 73.

14. Ibid., 89-90.

15. The centerpiece of Thaxton's attempt to delineate peasant mentality is a chapter entitled "Revolutionary Instructions from Below" which is based entirely upon a single novel published in China in 1962.

16. Some of these mistakes are pointed out in my review of Thaxton's book in *Pacific Affairs* (Fall 1983). Many more are detailed in Ch'en Yung-fa and Gregor Benton, *Moral Economy and the Chinese Revolution: A Critique*, (Amsterdam: University of Amsterdam Press, 1984).

17. Feng Tsu-ch'iung and Hou Te-fan, "Chan-sheng ti-chu wu-chuang Hung-ch'iang-hui te tou-cheng" [The struggle to defeat the landlords' military force, the Red Spears], in *Cheng-chou Ta-hsüeh Hsüeh-pao*, no. 1 (1980): 48-49.

18. This is Thaxton's characterization of Chinese peasant mentality; see Thaxton, *China Turned Rightside Up*, 230.

19. Joseph W. Esherick, "On the Social Origins of the Boxer Movement" (Paper presented to the International Conference on the Boxer Movement, Tsinan, Shantung, 14-20 November 1980).

20. Mitani, "Kokumin kakumei jiki no hoppō nōmin bōdō," 273.

21. Feng and Hou, "Chan-shen ti-chu wu-chuang," 48.

22. Sun Hsiu-shen, Chang Te-chung, Hsiao Chen-chung, and Nieh Yüan-ching, "Ho-nan Hua-hsien Hung-ch'iang-hui te fa-chan yü fu-mieh" [The development and demise of the Red Spears of Hua county, Honan], *Wen-shih tzu-liao hsüan-chi*, no. 47 (1980): 66-70.

23. Baba, "Kōsōkai undō josetsu," 120-38.

24. Baba, "Kōsokai," 71, 82.

25. Naquin, *Shantung Rebellion*, 100-101.

26. See *Hung-ch'i p'iao-p'iao* [The red flag flutters], vol. 3 (1957): 39-44; and Li Hsiao-ming, *P'ing-yüan ch'iang-sheng* [Rifle sounds on the plain] (Peking: Tso-chia ch'u-pan-she, 1965).

27. *Huang-Ma ch'i-i* [The Huang-Ma uprising] (Hupei: Jen-min ch'u-pan-she, 1978).

28. Ibid., 37, 98-100.

29. Ibid., 31-32.

30. Mitani, "Dentōteki nōmin tōsō no shintenkai," 142.

31. *Huang-Ma ch'i-i,* 100.
32. Feng and Hou, "Chan-sheng ti-chu wu-chuang," 52-53.
33. Sun, Chang, Hsiao, and Nieh, "Ho-nan Hua-hsien Hung-ch'iang-hui," 70-78.
34. See Perry, *Rebels and Revolutionaries,* 224-34.
35. For the late 1940s, see ibid., 235-39; and Ch'en Yung-fa, "The Wartime Communists and Their Local Rivals: Bandits and Secret Societies," in *Select Papers from the Center for Far Eastern Studies,* ed. Susan Mann Jones (Chicago: University of Chicago Press, 1979), 28, 36. For the 1950s, see Perry, *Rebels and Revolutionaries,* 258; and *Chieh-fang jih-pao* [Liberation daily], 5 June 1953, Shanghai, for a list of prohibited secret societies which includes the Red Spears.

Translator's Introduction

1. The biographical information was provided by Professor Tai in a personal communication to the translator.
2. Tai Hsüan-chih, *Yi-ho-t'uan yen-chiu* [Research on the Boxers] (Taipei: Chinese Commission for the Support of Scholarship, 1963); and *Hung-chiang-hui, 1916-1949* [The Red Spears, 1916-1949] (Taipei: Shih-huo Publishing Company, 1973).

   Three reviews of *The Red Spears* have been published to date. A brief and complimentary review is Sakai Tadao, "Tai Genji saku *Kōsōkai,*" in *Shakai bunkashi gaku,* 11 (1974): 50-53. It was translated into Chinese by Sung Ming-shun and appeared in *Shih-huo yüeh-k'an* 5, no. 2 (May 1975): 94-96.

   The book was reviewed in English, with comments on its content and interpretive line, by David D. Buck, *Journal of Asian Studies* 37, no. 4 (August 1977): 729-31.

   A lengthy review, which places the Red Spears in the context of conditions in China in the early decades of the twentieth century, is Baba Takeshi, "Kōsōkai: sono shiso to soshiki" [The Red Spears: the organization and ideology], *Shakai keizaishigaku,* 42, no. 1 (October 1978): 38-43.

Chapter I: Origins of the Red Spears

1. *Kuan-t'ao hsien-chih* [Gazetteer for Kuan-t'ao hsien], ed. Liu Ch'ing-ju (1936; reprint), section on "Politics."

2. See *Shan-tung chün-hsing chi-lei* [A record of the military in Shantung] (reprint, Taiwan: Ch'eng-wen Publishing Company), *chüan* 22, "Bandits," pt. 1.
3. Ibid.
4. Ibid.
5. Ibid.
6. Ibid.
7. Kuo Ting-yi, *Chin-tai Chung-kuo shih-shih jih-chi* [A chronological record of modern Chinese history] (Taipei: n.p., 1963), 212.
8. *Ch'ao-ch'eng hsien-chih* [Gazetteer for Ch'ao-ch'eng hsien], ed. Chao Ch'ang (1920), *chüan* 1, "Military System."
9. *Shan-tung chün-hsing chi-lei*, *chüan* 22, "Bandits," pt. 1.
10. Ibid., pt. 2.
11. Ibid., pt. 3.
12. Ibid., pt. 2.
13. Ibid.
14. Ibid.
15. Ibid., pt. 3.
16. *Hsü Wu-chih hsien-chih* [Gazetteer for Wu-chih hsien, continued], ed. Shih Yen-shou (1921), *chüan* 24.
17. *Tung-ming hsien-chih* [Gazetteer for Tung-ming hsien], ed. Jen Chuan-tsao (1933), *chüan* 11, "Local Notables." See also *Shan-tung chün-hsing chi-lei*, *chüan* 22.
18. *Kuan hsien-chih* [Gazetteer for Kuan-hsien], ed. Chao Hsi-shu (1933), "On the Li-yüan-t'un Sect."
19. *Chang-ko hsien-chih* [Gazetteer for Ch'ang-ko hsien], ed. Chang Chai-ts'un (1930), *chüan* 3.
20. See *Hsing-yüan ju-jen* [Master of the Hsing Garden], *Chung-yüan tsai-huo yu-t'ien-lu* [A record of the catastrophies on the central plain] (Taipei: Chung-hsing p'ing-lun-she, 1968), 144.
21. *Kuang-shan hsien-chih-kao* [A draft gazetteer for Kuang-shan hsien], ed. Ch'ao T'iao-p'ing (1936), "Chronological Record."
22. *Hsü An-yang hsien-chih* [Gazetteer for An-yang hsien, continued], ed. Fang Tse-chu (1933), *chüan* 1, "Chronological Record."
23. Ibid., *chüan* 9, "Military Defense."
24. Chang Chen-chih, *Ke-ming yü tsung-chiao* [Revolution and religion] (Shanghai: Min-chih, 1929), 132.
25. *Hsing-yüan ju-jen*, 143-44.
26. Ibid.

27. *Yen-ling hsien-chih* [Gazetteer for Yen-ling hsien], ed. Wang Chieh (1936), *chüan* 1, "Chronological Record."
28. *Hsi-p'ing hsien-chih* [Gazetteer for Hsi-p'ing hsien], ed. Ch'en Ming-chien (1934), *chüan* 14, "Military Defense."

Chapter II: Modern China and the Red Spears

1. *Min-kuo ching-shih wen-p'ien* [Essays on the Republican period] (reprint, Taiwan: Wen-hsing shu-tien). See "Internal Government," no. 4.
2. *Hsü An-yang hsien-chih, chüan* 1, "Chronological Record."
3. Ibid., *chüan* 10, "On Society."
4. *Hsin-ho hsien-chih* [Gazetteer for Hsin-ho hsien], ed. Chuan Chen-lun (1928), "Local Areas."
5. *Han-tan hsien-chih* [Gazetteer for Han-tan hsien], ed. Pi Hsing-tan (1933), *chüan* 6, "Local Areas."
6. *Hsin-ho hsien-chih*, "Local Areas."
7. *Hsü An-yang hsien-chih, chüan* 10, "Society."
8. *Chung-hsiu Hsin-yang hsien-chih* [Revised gazetteer for Hsin-yang hsien], ed. Ch'en Hsiang-t'ung, *chüan* 17.
9. *Kuan hsien-chih, chüan* 6, "Local Areas."
10. *Hsü An-yang hsien-chih, chüan* 10, "Society."
11. *Chin-hsien chih-liao* [Gazetteer for Chin-hsien], ed. P'eng Hsi-hsin (1934), "Customs." See also *Mi-hsien chih* [Gazetteer for Mi-hsien], ed. Wang Chung (1923), *chüan* 6, "Local Areas."
12. *Ch'eng-an hsien-chih* [Gazetteer for Ch'eng-an hsien], ed. Chang Yung-ho (1931), *chüan* 15, "Stories."
13. Ibid.
14. K'ang Hsüan-i, *Ch'uan-cheng chien-shih* [A brief history of the wars in Szechuan]. See the special issue of *Fu-hsing Monthly*.
15. Wen Kung-chih, *Tsui-chin san-shih-nien Chung-kuo chün-shih shih* [A history of China's military during the past thirty years], vol. 2, (Taiwan: Wen-hsing shu-tien, n.d.): 427.
16. Ibid., 132.
17. Ibid., 160.
18. Ibid., 184.
19. Ibid., 188.
20. Han Sheng, "Chung-kuo nung-min tan-fu te fu-shui" [The taxes borne by the Chinese peasants], *Tung-fang tsa-chih* [Eastern miscellany] (October 1928).
21. Ibid.

22. Wen, *Chung-kuo chün-shih shih*, vol. 1, 160.
23. *Kuang-tsung hsien-chih* [Gazetteer for Kuang-tsung hsien], ed. Han Mei-hsiu (1933), *chüan* 7, "Financial Affairs"; *Han-tan hsien-chih*, *chüan* 1, "Chronological History."
24. Ibid., *chüan* 3, "Daily Life."
25. *Tung-ming hsien-hsin-chih* [New gazetteer for Tung-ming hsien], ed. Jen Chuan-tsao and Mu Hsiang-chung (1933), *chüan* 18, "The Military."
26. Ibid., *chüan* 20.
27. Ibid., *chüan* 7, "Population Records."
28. Ibid., *chüan* 13, "Life."
29. *Wang-tou hsien-chih* [Gazetteer for Wang-tou hsien], ed. Ts'ui Lien-fen (1934), *chüan* 3; *chüan* 10, "Local Customs."
30. *Ching-hsien chih* [Gazetteer for Ching-hsien], ed. Chang Ju-yi (1931), *chüan* 14, "Historical Events."
31. *Han-tan hsien-chih*, *chüan* 1, "Historical Records."
32. *Hsü An-yang hsien-chih*, *chüan* 1, "Chronological Record." [Fifty-one examples of taxes are listed in Tai's original text.]
33. Yung Lo, "Chang Tsung-ch'ang huo-lu-chih" [A record of Chang Tsung-ch'ang's rape of Shantung], part 2, *Mien-ching Magazine*, no. 6.
34. Ibid.
35. Chung Chih, "Chang Tsung-ch'ang huo-lu-chi" [A record of Chang Tsung-ch'ang's rape of Shantung], part 1, *Mien-ching Magazine*, no. 5.
36. Ibid., part 3, no. 7.
37. Shou Yu, "Chih-hsi yu-nieh tui Ho-nan min-chung chih po-hsüeh" [Crimes of the Chihli clique against the people of Honan], *Hsiang-tao Weekly*, no. 186.
38. "Chih-hsi chün-fa ma-ti-hsia te Shan-tung jen-min" [The people of Shantung under control of the Chihli clique], *Hsiang-tao Weekly*, no. 88.
39. Chao Shan, "Sun Chun-fang chün-shih ju-lan hsia chih Che-chiang" [Chekiang trampled by Sun Chun-fang's forces], *Hsiang-tao Weekly*, no. 185.
40. *Tung-fang tsa-chih*, (August 1917).
41. *P'ing-shan hsien-chih-liao* [Materials for the gazetteer of P'ing-shan hsien], "Hopei, Customs," no. 4, "Folk Songs."
42. *Tung-ming hsien hsin-chih*, *chüan* 18, "Military Affairs."
43. *Hsü An-yang hsien-chih*, *chüan* 1, "Chronological Record."
44. *Hsin-yang hsien-chih* [Gazetteer for Hsin-yang hsien], ed. Ch'en Shan-t'ung (1936), *chüan* 18, "Military Affairs."

45. *P'ing-shan hsien-chih-liao*, "Historical Accounts," 15.
46. *Shih-ho hsien-chih*, "On Customs, Contemporary Society."
47. Liu Ta-chün, "Chung-kuo nung-t'ien t'ung-chih" [Computing Chinese agricultural fields], *Chung-kuo ching-chi wen-t'i* [Chinese economic problems].
48. *Han-tan hsien-chih, chüan* 6, "Local Customs."
49. *Kuang-tsung hsien-chih, chüan* 4, "Local Customs."
50. *Tung-ming hsien-hsin-chih, chüan* 13, "Daily Life."
51. *Kuang-tsung hsien-chih, chüan* 4, "Local Customs."
52. *Tung-ming hsien-chih, chüan* 13, "Daily Life."
53. *Hsü An-yang hsien-chih, chüan* 10, "Society."
54. *Tung-p'ing hsien-chih* [Gazetteer of Tung-p'ing hsien], ed. Liu Ch'ing-yu (1935), *chüan* 5, "Customs, Daily Life." See also *Han-tan hsien-chih, chüan* 7.
55. *Wang-tou hsien-chih, chüan* 10, "Customs."
56. *Ta-ming hsien-chih* [Gazetteer for Ta-ming hsien], ed. Jen Chao-lien (1934), *chüan* 26.
57. *Hsin-ho hsien-chih*, "Chronological Record."
58. Ibid., "Local Customs."
59. *Nan-kung hsien-chih* [Gazetteer for Nan-kung hsien], ed. Chia En-fu (1936), *chüan* 24.
60. *Tung-fang tsa-chih* (August 1925).
61. Ibid., vol. 26, no. 12.
62. See "Memorial from Teng Hsiao-chin to the Szechuan Provincial Relief Society," 1936.
63. *Hsin-tu pao* [New independent news], 24 March 1936.
64. *Fu-hsing jih-pao* [Revival daily news], 21 March 1936.
65. Report from *Pei-ch'uan*, dated 18 March 1936; see the memorial by Teng Hsiao-chin.
66. *Fu-hsing jih-pao*, 21 March 1936; *Chen-wu hsün-k'an* [Bimonthly relief news], no. 23.
67. Han, "Chung-kuo nung-min."
68. See *Tung-fang tsa-chih*, 24, no. 16; see also Han, "Chung-kuo nung-min."
69. Ibid.
70. Ibid.
71. *T'an-wu t'u-lieh yü Sze-ch'uan nung-ts'un* [The avaricious gentry and Szechuan's peasant villages], 130; Huang Yen-p'ei, *Tu-tao* [The independent road] (Shanghai: K'ai-ming shu-tien, 1948), 91.
72. Ibid.
73. *Chin hsien-chin, chüan* 1, "Customs."

74. *Lin-ch'ing hsien-chih* [Gazetteer for Lin-ch'ing hsien], ed. Chang Shu-mei (1934), "Customs," no. 8, "Folk Sayings."
75. Huang, *Tu-tao*, 90.
76. Ibid., 92.
77. Ibid., 202.
78. Ibid., 190.
79. Cheng Chen-chih, *Mu-ch'ien Chung-kuo she-hui te ping-t'ai* [The current sickness of Chinese society] (Shanghai: Min-chih shu-tien, 1929), 140-48.
80. Ibid., 158-59.
81. Shu Chih, "Chün-fa t'ung-chih-hsia chih tsai-huang yü mi-huang" [Calamities and catastrophies under the warlords], *Hsiang-tao Weekly*, no. 164.
82. *Hsin-yang hsien-chih*, *chüan* 11; *Ch'ing-p'ing hsien-chih* [Gazetteer for Ch'ing-p'ing hsien], ed. Chang Shu-mei (1935), "Economy and Currency."
83. Chang, *Ke-ming yü tsung-chiao*, 153; *Hsü An-yang hsien-chih*, *chüan* 9, "Military Defense."
84. *Nan-kung hsien-chih*, *chüan* 22; *Ch'ing-ch'eng hsien-chih* [Gazetteer for Ch'ing-ch'eng hsien], "Military Affairs."
85. Ho Hsi-ya, *Chung-kuo t'u-fei wen-t'i chih yen-chiu* [Research on China's bandit problem] (Shanghai: T'ai-tung tu-shu-chu, 1925), 66.
86. Ibid.
87. *Chung-hsiu Lin-hsien chih* [Revised gazetteer for Lin-hsien], ed. Li Chien-ch'uan (1932), *chüan* 14, "Chronological Chart."
88. *Yen-ling hsien-chih*, *chüan* 1, "Chronological History."
89. *Cheng-yang hsien-chih*, *chüan* 3.
90. *T'ai-ho hsien-chih* [Gazetteer for T'ai-ho hsien], ed. Ting Ping-liang (1920), *chüan* 6, "Military Reserves and Military Affairs."
91. *Ch'üeh-shan hsien-chih* [Gazetteer for Ch'üeh-shan hsien], ed. Li Ching-t'ang (1931), *chüan* 20, "Chronological Record."
92. *Yen-ling hsien-chih*, *chüan* 1, "Chronological Record."
93. Ibid.
94. *Ch'ang-mu hsien-chih* [Gazetteer for Ch'ang-mu hsien], ed. Chang Chi-ts'un (1932 reprint), *chüan* 3.
95. Ho, *Chung-kuo t'u-fei*, 70; *Kuang-tsun hsien-chih*, *chüan* 3.
96. *Yang-hsin hsien-chih* [Gazetteer for Yang-hsin hsien], ed. Chu Lan (1926), *chüan* 4, "Military Affairs."
97. Ho, *Chung-kuo t'u-fei*, 50.

98. Ibid., 39-41.

99. Nagano Akira, *Dohi, guntai, kōsōkai* [Bandits, the military, and the Red Spears] (Tokyo: 1931), 23.

100. *Tung-ming hsien hsin-chih, chüan* 20, "Bandits."

101. *Yu hsien-chih, chüan* 2, "Chronological Record."

102. *Kuang-tsun hsien-chih, chüan* 3, "People's Lives."

103. *T'ai-k'ang hsien-chih* [Gazetteer for T'ai-k'ang hsien], ed. Liu P'an-sui (1933), *chüan* 10, "Noted People."

104. *Ting-hsien chih* [Gazetteer for Ting-hsien], ed. Lu Fu (1934), *chüan* 17, "Military Affairs."

105. T'ien Jan, "Wu-hsi chün-fa t'ung-chih-hsia Ching-te" [Ching-te under the warlord control of the Wu clique], *Hsiang-tao Weekly*, no. 168.

106. Ibid.

107. Chang Chieh-hou, "Huai-pei nung-min chih sheng-huo hsing-kuang" [Conditions of peasant life in northern Anhwei], *Tung-fang tsa-chih* 24, no. 16.

108. *Lin-ch'ing hsien-chih, chüan* 8, "Customs."

109. Ho, *Chung-kuo t'u-fei*, 89.

110. *Hsin-yang hsien-chih, chüan* 19, "Military Affairs."

111. *Yang-wu hsien-chih* [Gazetteer for Yang-wu hsien], ed. Keng Pei (1936), *chüan* 1, "Military Reserves."

112. Jen Chuan-tsao, *Chih-fei chi-lüeh* [Bandit incursions] (Taipei: Wen-hai Publishing Company, 1960), 2.

113. Suo Huai, "Ho-nan chün-shih hsing-kuang yü cheng-chih ch'ien-tu" [The military situation in Honan and future military events]. *Hsiang-tao Weekly*, no. 169.

114. *Ch'ing-ho hsien-chih* [Gazetteer for Ch'ing-ho hsien], ed. Wang T'ung-chia (1933), *chuan* 6.

115. *Ta-ming hsien-chih, chüan* 12, "Military Affairs"; *Kuang-shan hsien chih-kao*, "Military Affairs."

116. *Kuang-tsung hsien-chih, chüan* 4, "Customs."

117. See Szu-ma Ch'ien, *Shih Chi* [Record of history].

118. *Hsin-ho hsien-chih*, "Customs."

Chapter III: Organization and Beliefs

1. Chang, *Ke-ming yü tsung-chiao*, 140. [In this translation the word "unit" does not usually refer to any specific military term, but simply means a group of secret-society members.]

2. Chi Fan, "Chieh-shao Ho-nan te hung-ch'iang hui" [Introducing the Red Spears of Honan], *Chung-kuo ch'ing-nien* [Chinese youth], 4, no. 1.
3. *Cheng-yang hsien-chih, chüan* 3, "Chronological Record."
4. Chang, *Ke-ming yü tsung-chiao*, 144.
5. Shen Shin, "Ho-nan chih hung-ch'iang hui" [The Red Spears of Honan], *Kuo-wen chou-pao* [Kuo-wen weekly], 4, no. 24.
6. Hsiang Yün-lung, "Hung-ch'iang hui te ch'i-yüan chi ch'i shan-hou" [Origin and activities of the Red Spears], *Tung-fang tsa-chih* 24, no. 21.
7. Shen, "Ho-nan chih hung-ch'iang hui." [The Chinese-language version includes a chart listing the names of sixty-three secret-society leaders and the numbers of men they commanded.]
8. Hsiang, "Hung-ch'iang hui te ch'i-yüan."
9. Wo Yu, "Hung-ch'iang hui chih nei-jung" [Affairs of the Red Spears], *Kuo-wen chou-pao* 4, no. 28.
10. Ch'ang Jung-te was a native of Kuang-tung hsien, Hopei province, and graduated from Peking University. He organized a Red Spears group in 1927 at the request of the central government and his organization battled the northern warlords.
11. Shen, "Ho-nan chih hung-ch'iang hui."
12. Chang, *Ke-ming yü tsung-chiao*, 142.
13. Hsiang, "Hung-ch'iang hui te ch'i-yüan."
14. Suemitsu Takayoshi, *Shina no himitsu kessha to jizen kessha* [China's secret societies and benevolent organizations] (Dairen: South Manchuria Railway Company, 1932).
15. *Hsü An-yang hsien-chih, chüan* 1.
16. *Ling-hsien hsü-chih* [Gazetteer for Lin-hsien, continued], ed. Miao En-p'o (1935), *chüan* 4, "Miscellaneous Events." See also Shen, "Ho-nan chih hung-ch'iang hui"; "Hung-ch'iang hui te ch'i-yüan."
17. Shen, "Ho-nan chih hung-ch'iang hui."
18. Wo, "Hung-ch'iang hui chih nei-jung"; "Hung ch'iang hui te ch'i-yüan."
19. Suemitsu, *Shina no himitsu*, 125.

Chapter IV: Ceremonies and Ritual Practices

1. *Tung-p'ing hsien-chih* [Gazetteer for Tung-p'ing hsien], ed. Liu Ch'ing-yu (1935), *chüan* 16, "Major Events."

2. "Hung-ch'iang-hui suo-kung-feng-te shen-p'ai-wei" [A spirit plaque worshipped by the Red Spears], *Pekin Mantetsu chōsa geppo* [Monthly research report of the South Manchurian Railway Company in Peking] 4, no. 5: 43.
3. "Hung-ch'iang kuan-hsi chi" [Records of the practices of the Red Spears], *Kuo-wen chou-pao* 5, no. 5.
4. Shen, "Ho-nan chih hung-ch'iang hui."
5. "Hung-ch'iang kuan-hsi chi."
6. Wang Meng-yang, *P'ing-chu yin-shih-p'u* [An annotated cookbook] (Taipei: Chung-kuo i-hsüeh ch'u-p'an-she, 1964).
7. Shen, "Ho-nan chih hung-ch'iang hui." [Tai goes on to discuss these schools in slightly more detail.]
8. Ibid.
9. See Liu Ta-chih, *Chung-kuo i-wu tu-shuo* [Illustrated guide to Chinese medicine], 217.
10. Chang, *Ke-ming yü tsung-chiao*, 171.
11. The "tiger's mouth" referred to a way of using the hands.
12. Chang, *Ke-ming yü tsung-chiao*, 136-37.
13. Wang Yung-jen, "Ta-tao hui" [The Big Sword Society], *Mien-ching Magazine*, no. 25.
14. Wo, "Hung-ch'iang hui chih nei-jung."
15. Well water was considered "yin" and river water was considered "yang." When mixed they were called "yin-yang water."
16. Chang, *Ke-ming yü tsung-chiao*, 138.
17. See the *Chung-kuo i-yao* [Journal of Chinese medicine] (May 1959).
18. In "opening the eyes" and "suspending sight," the initiate listened with his eyes closed.
19. Carts used in north China were often four-wheeled and could weigh as much as three thousand *chin*; some were even meant to be pulled by three or four horses.
20. The record of this ceremony is in Yang Lien-sheng, "Tsou-huo-chi" [A record of walking on coal], original manuscript in the possession of the author.
21. Wang, "Ta-tao hui." [Tai includes illustrations of these amulets.]
22. Contributed by a former Red Spears member.
23. This was a basic chant, to be spoken repeatedly but silently.
24. Suemitsu, *Shina no himitsu*, 134.
25. Ibid. [Tai gives thirteen examples of magic formulae used by Red Spears members which are not translated here.]
26. *Hsi-p'ing hsien-chih*, chüan 34.

27. These were known as *ch'u hsieh*, and were designed to chase away the devils, called *hsieh*, meaning "evil" or "vicious."

Chapter V: Offshoots of the Red Spears

1. Amulets were divided into two classes, the "fresh" and the "cooked." Cooked amulets were burned and the ashes drunk with water. Fresh amulets were eaten whole after burning.
2. The right hand was considered evil because it could be used to kill and because it was often used after urinating or defecating.
3. [Tai includes further descriptions of forbidden foods. Some of the prohibitions are derived from Buddhism and others from religious Taoism.]
4. *Hsü An-yang hsien-chih, chüan* 1, "Chronological Record."
5. Ibid.
6. Nagano, *Dohi, guntai, kōsōkai,* 255.
7. Special names were given to the fingers. For example, the index, middle, and ring fingers were called the "three mountains."
8. [Further discussion of these ceremonies may be found in the Chinese-language version.]
9. This was revealed to me by a former member of the White Spears, named Chang Chung-hsi, from Shantung province.
10. *Hsing-yüan ju-jen* [Master of the Strange Garden], 145.
11. Suemitsu, *Shina no himitsu,* 145.
12. Chang, *Ke-ming yü tsung-chiao,* 147.
13. *Hsing-yüan ju-jen,* 145.
14. Memorial from Governor Li Ping-heng of Shantung, dated 24 June 1897.
15. Telegram from Li Ping-heng, dated 28 June 1898.
16. See Wu Hsüan-i, trans., *K'ang-tzu Yi-ho-t'uan yün-tung shih-mo* [The Boxer movement of 1900].
17. *Cheng-yang hsien-chih, chüan* 3, "Chronological Record."
18. *Tsung-hsiu Chiao-chih* [Revised and enlarged gazetteer for Chia-hsien], ed. Chao Wen-yün (1931), *chüan* 33, "Military Affairs."
19. Suemitsu, *Shina no himitsu,* 149.
20. Chang, *Ke-ming-yü tsung-chiao,* 186.
21. See ibid., 173; and Suemitsu, *Shina no himitsu,* 150-51.
22. Suemitsu, *Shina no himitsu,* 159.
23. Ibid., 174.

24. Chang, *Ke-ming yü tsung-chiao*, 161-62.
25. Chang, *Mu-ch'ien Chung-kuo she-hui*, 157.
26. Ibid.; see also Chang, *Ke-ming yü tsung-chiao*, 157-58.
27. Chang, *Ke-ming yü tsung-chiao*, 153.
28. See the *Chung-shan jih-pao* [Chung-shan daily news], from Hankou, 7 May 1928.
29. Chang, *Ke-ming yü tsung-chiao*, 153-54.
30. Ibid., 163-65.
31. See the article in *Ch'eng-tu pai-jih hsin-wen* [Chengtu daily news], 19 October 1928.
32. Hsin Min, "Chieh-shao Sze-ch'uan i-fu liu-min-tu" [A picture introducing the homeless of Szechuan], *Tu-tao Magazine*, no. 3.
33. *Yen-ling hsien-chih*, chüan 1, "Chronological Record."
34. *Tzu-ch'ing shih-ch'ao sheng-hsün* [Sacred instructions from the Ch'ing emperor] (reprint, Taipei: Wen-hai Ch'u-pan-she), chüan 82.
35. Chang, *Ke-ming yü tsung-chiao*, 135.
36. See the *Ta-ming hsien-chih*, chüan 12; *Chung-hsiu lin hsien-chih*, chüan 14; and Wang Jao-ming, "Hung-ch'iang hui wo-men-te chiao-hsün" [The lesson taught to us by the Red Spears], *Pei-ching ch'en-pao* [Peking morning news], 4 February 1927.
37. *Chung-hsiu lin-hsien chih*, chüan 17.
38. Ibid.
39. Ibid.
40. *Hsü An-yang hsien-chih*, chüan 1.
41. Wang, "Hung-ch'iang hui wo-men-te chiao-hsün."
42. Hsiang, "Hung-ch'iang hui te ch'i-yüan."
43. *Chung-hsiu Lin hsien-chih*, chüan 17, "Miscellaneous."
44. Ibid.
45. Tzu Chen, "Fan-feng chan-cheng chung chih yü-pei t'ien-men hui" [The Heavenly Gate Society in northern Honan opposing the Feng-tien war], *Hsiang-tao Weekly*, no. 197.
46. See Suemitsu, *Shina no himitsu*, 193.
47. Tzu Chen, "Fan-feng chan-cheng."
48. One such slogan used was "Food for Everyone, Drink for Everyone."
49. Yüan Ching-yao, "T'ai-ch'i-tao te kai-lei" [An outline of the T'ai-chi-tao], manuscript in the author's possession.
50. Nagano, *Dohi, guntai, kōsōkai*, 256.
51. Suemitsu, *Shina no himitsu*, 194.
52. Chang, *Ke-ming yü tsung-chiao*, 188.

53. Li Han-san, "Wu-chi tao" [The effortless way], manuscript in the author's possession.
54. Chang, *Ke-ming yü tsung-chiao*, 189.
55. Ibid., 109.
56. Many such incidents are recorded for Shantung. See *Chi-tung hsien-chih* [Gazetteer for Chi-tung hsien] (1935), *chüan* 2.
57. Su Wen-chi, "Lu-hsi k'uai-tao" [The K'uai-Tao sect in western Shantung], manuscript in the author's possession.
58. Ibid.
59. *Kuan hsien-chih*, *chüan* 10.
60. *Han-tan hsien-chih*, *chüan* 4, "Government."
61. *Ke-ming K'ung-ch'i mi-man-chung chih Ho-nan* [The revolutionary wind in flooded Honan].
62. Ch'un Feng, "Tung-pei i-yung chün" [The northeast volunteer corps], *Mien-ching Magazine*, no. 24.
63. *Hsü An-yang hsien-chih*, *chüan* 9, "Military Defense."
64. *Lai-yang hsien-chih* [Gazetteer for Lai-yang hsien], ed. Chang Chung-chun (1935), *chüan* 2-1.
65. *Hsia-chin hsien-chih* [Gazetteer for Hsia-chin hsien], ed. Liang Ta-k'un (1934), extra volume, *chüan* 2, "Military System under the Republic."
66. *Tung-p'ing hsien-chih*, *chüan* 7, "Government Affairs."
67. *Hsia-chin hsien-chih*, extra volume, *chüan* 2.
68. Ibid.
69. *Tung-p'ing hsien-chih*, *chüan* 7.
70. *Kuan-t'ao hsien-chih*, "Government," no. 9.
71. *Yeh-hsien chih* [Gazetteer for Yeh-hsien], *chüan* 3, "Police."
72. *Kuan-t'ao hsien-chih*, *chüan* 9. [Tai provides the details here.]
73. *Ch'ing-p'ing hsien-chih*, volume on "Events, Ceremonies."
74. *Hsia-chin hsien-chih*, extra volume, *chüan* 2.
75. *Chan-hua hsien-chih* [Gazetteer for Chan-hua hsien], ed. Yu Ch'ing-p'an (1936), *chüan* 7.
76. *Chi-tung hsien-chih* [Gazetteer for Chi-tung hsien], ed. Yu Ch'ing-p'an (1935), *chüan* 4.
77. *Hsü An-yang hsien-chih*, *chüan* 1; *Han-tan hsien-chih*, *chüan* 1.
78. Suemitsu, *Shina no himitsu*, 189.
79. Chang, *Ke-ming yü tsung-chiao*.
80. Nagano, *Dohi, guntai, kōsōkai*, 260.
81. Chang, *Ke-ming yü tsung-chiao*, 149.
82. *Yu hsien-chih*, *chüan* 2.
83. Ibid.

84. *Yen-ling hsien-chih, chüan* 1. [Tai goes on to describe thirty-nine other secret societies.]

Chapter VI: Transformation of the Red Spears

1. Hsiang, "Hung-ch'iang hui te ch'i-yüan."
2. *Kuang-tsung hsien-chih, chüan* 4; *Mi hsien-chih, chüan* 6.
3. *Yüan-shih hsien-chih* [Gazetteer for Yüan-shih hsien], ed. Li Lin-kuei (1931), "Customs and Folk Songs."
4. Chang, *Ke-ming yü tsung-chiao*, 157-58.
5. The secretary was often called the *shih-yeh* [elder master] in accordance with Ch'ing usage.
6. Chang, *Ke-ming yü tsung-chiao*, 144.
7. Chi, "Chieh-shao Ho-nan te hung-ch'iang hui."
8. *Hua-hsien hsien-chih* [Gazetteer for Hua-hsien], ed. Wang P'u-yüan], *chüan* 20, "Chronological Record," section "On the Red Spears."
9. *Hsü An-yang hsien-chih, chüan* 1.
10. *P'ing-shan hsien-chih-liao, chüan* 10.
11. *Meng-hsien chih* [Gazetteer for Meng-hsien], ed. Sung Li-yu (1933), *chüan* 4.
12. *Ling-hsien hsü-chih, chüan* 4.
13. Shen, "Ho-nan chih hung-ch'iang hui."
14. Hsiang, "Hung-ch'iang hui te ch'i-yüan."
15. *Tung-p'ing hsien-chih, chüan* 5, "Folk Songs."
16. Shan Yü, "Chih-nan yü-pei min-chung fan-k'ang Feng-chün ch'ing-hsing" [Popular resistance to the Feng-tien Army in southern Chihli and northern Honan], *Hsiang-tao Weekly*, no. 188. See also Shou, "Chih-hsi yu-nieh."
17. *Ling-hsien hsü-chih, chüan* 4.
18. *Hsin-yang hsien-chih, chüan* 18.
19. *Cheng-yang hsien-chih, chüan* 3.
20. Ibid.
21. *Hsin-an hsien-chih* [Gazetteer for Hsin-an hsien], ed. Li Hsi-pai (1938), *chüan* 1.
22. See *Ta-ming hsien-chih, chüan* 12.
23. *Ju-nan hsien-chih* [Gazetteer for Ju-nan hsien], ed. Li Huo-yün (revised edition; 1938), *chüan* 15.
24. *Hsü An-yang hsien-chih, chüan* 1.
25. *Chiao chih*, ed. Chao Wen-yün, et. al. (1930), *chüan* 33, "Military and Military Defense."

26. *Lin-ch'u hsien hsü-chih* [Gazetteer for Lin-ch'u hsien, continued], ed. Liu Jen-yu (1935), *chüan* 1-2, "Chronological Record."

27. Jen Ching, "Ho-nan Lu-shih hsien jen-min tui chün-fa chih fan-k'ang" [The people of Lu-shih hsien in Honan oppose the warlords], *Hsiang-tao Weekly*, no. 69.

28. "Hsiao-shih-hua ta-te An-hui fei-luan" [The insignificant but important bandit problem in Anhwei], *Tung-fang tsa-chih* 21, no. 14.

29. *Ch'üeh-shan hsien-chih*, *chüan* 20, "Record of Important Events."

30. *Ch'eng-an hsien-chih*, *chüan* 15, "Stories."

31. [In a portion of the text not translated here, a total of thirteen examples are given from the provinces of Shantung, Honan, Hopei, Anhwei, Hupei, and Szechuan, between 1923 and 1928.]

32. *Hua-hsien hsien-chih*, *chüan* 20. The *Yüan-shih hsien-chih* includes a discussion of the Red Spears.

33. *Kao-pa hsien-chih* [Gazetteer for Kao-pa hsien], ed. Sung Wen-hua (1931), *chüan* 10, "Stories."

34. *Ch'üeh-shan hsien-chih*, *chüan* 20, "Chronological Record."

35. *Hsin-ho hsien-chih*, "Record of Important Events."

36. *Nan-kung hsien-chih*, *chüan* 22.

37. This event is reported in the *T'ien-chin ta kung-pao*, 24 November 1927.

38. See *Ke-ming yü tsung-chiao*, 142.

39. "A mouthful" was another term for a solder, deriving from the fact that every soldier has to be fed.

40. For Hopei, see the *Hsin-ho hsien-chih*, "Customs and Folk Songs." For Honan, see *Hsü An-yang hsien-chih*, *chüan* 10.

41. See ibid., *chüan* 9; and Wen, *Tsui-chin san-shih-nien Chung-kuo chün-shin shih*, 142.

42. This sytem had other names such as "Buying a Substitute."

43. China was divided into a number of military areas for administrative purposes. Each area was responsible for recruiting troops and seeing that they were trained.

44. Huang, *Tu-tao*.

45. One source estimates that two-thirds of the Chinese population of Singapore were deserters or others evading conscription. See the *Hsin-cha-p'o hua-tzu ts'un-shih tiao-ch'a pao-kao* [Report on the investigation of Chinese villages in Singapore] (1969).

46. *Hsing-yüan chu-jen*, 181.

47. Several stars would be woven in black thread on a yellow flag.

48. *Ch'uan-fei chi-shih, chüan* 4, contains a report by a Japanese officer named Sawara Atsuaki, a member of the International Relief Force formed to oppose the Boxers.
49. *Tung-p'ing hsien-chih, chüan* 16, "Important Events."

Chapter VII: Accomplishments of the Red Spears

1. Kao Wei-yo, "Su-lien yin-mou wen-teng hui-p'ien" [Document on Soviet plotting] (1928, mimeographed). See the section, "Politics."
2. Ibid., "The Kuo-min Army," 20.
3. Ibid.
4. Ibid.
5. Tuo Hsiu, "Hung-ch'iang-hui yü Chung-kuo te nung-min pao-tung" [The Red Spears and the Chinese peasant uprisings], *Hsiang-tao Weekly*, no. 158.
6. Li Ta-chao, "Lu-Yu-Shen teng-sheng-te hung-ch'iang hui" [The Red Spears in Shantung, Hopei, Shensi, and other provinces], in *Li Ta-chao hsüan-chi* [Collected works of Li Ta-chao], 565-66.
7. Ibid., 566.
8. Ibid., 567.
9. Ibid., 569-70.
10. Kao, "Su-lien yin-mou wen-teng hui-p'ien," "Chinese Communist Party," 53-54.
11. Record of the KMT Central Political Committee in Wuhan, 28 March 1927.
12. Record of the KMT Central Administrative Committee in Wuhan, Second Conference, 22 March 1927.
13. Record of the KMT Central Peasant's Movement Committee in Wuhan, 26 April 1927.
14. Record of the KMT Central Peasant's Department, Twelfth Conference, 9 July 1927.
15. See Chiang Yung-ching, *Bo-lo-yen yü Wu-han ching-ch'uan* [Borodin and the Wuhan regime], 374-75.
16. Record of the KMT Central Peasant's Department in Wuhan, Eleventh Departmental Meeting, 1 July 1927.
17. Ibid. See also Record of the KMT Central Political Committee in Wuhan, Twenty-sixth Meeting, 1 July 1927.
18. Wen, *Ts'ui-chin san-shih-nien Chung-kuo chün-shih shih*, vol. 1, 184; Kao, "Su-lien yin-mou wen-teng hui-p'ien," "Kuo-min Army," 28-29.

19. See the Red Spears public announcment quoted in chapter 6, page 91.
20. Shen Chou, "Kuo-min-chün ti-erh-chün chih shih-pai" [Defeat of the Second Kuomin Army], *Hsiang-tao Weekly*, no. 147.
21. Chi Fan, "Chieh-shao Ho-nan te hung-ch'iang hui"; see also *Shen-hsien chih* [Gazetteer for Shen-hsien], ed. Kuo Ching-shou (1936) *chüan* 1, "Record of Important Events."
22. Shou, "Chih-hsi yu-nieh."
23. Chang, *Ke-ming yü tsung-chiao*, 145.
24. In addition to the sources quoted in this section, see Wen, "Chung-kuo chün-shih shih," vol. 2, 321-27; and *Shih-an hsien-chih*, *chüan* 1.

Glossary

an-kung 安宮

An-lu hsien 安陸縣

An-yang hsien 安陽縣

Anhwei 安徽

bushido 武士道

Ch'ai Fu-chih 柴福智

Chan-ch'u nung-min yün-tung
  wei-yüan hui 戰區農民
運動委員會

Chang (river) 澎河

Chang Ch'en 張陳

Chang ch'i 張其

Ch'ang-ch'i-chiang 常旗將

Chang Chia-to 張家鐸

Chang Chien-yang 張建陽

Chang Chih-kung 張治公

Chang Ching-hsiu 張景修

Chang Ching-wang 張景旺

Chang Chung-hsi 張中喜

Chang Fei 張飛

Chang Feng-tzu 張瘋子

Chang Hsüeh-liang 張學良

Ch'ang-ko hsien 長葛縣

Chang K'ung-wu 張工五

Chang Kuo-hsin 張國信

Chang Li-shan 張立山

Chang Liang-chi 張亮基

Chang Meng-hu 張猛虎

Chang Mo-ching 張莫京

Ch'ang-sheng-chün 長勝軍

Chang Shih-chi 張士奇

Chang-te 彰德、

Chang Ting-fu 張鼎輔

Chang Ting-shan 張定山

Chang Tso-lin 張作霖

137

Chang Tsung-ch'ang 張宗昌

Chang Tzu-heng 張子亨

Chang Wen-hsüeh 張文學

Chang Yao-ch'ang 張耀昶

Ch'ang-yüan hsien 長垣縣

Ch'ang Yung-te 長榮德

Chao Ch'eng-ch'iu 趙成秋

Chao Chün-ling 趙俊嶺

chao-kung 抓功

Chao Shang-chih 趙尚志

Chao Shu-hsün 趙樹勳

chen 鎮

Ch'en Ch'iao 陳橋

ch'en-fu yu szu-hai 朕富有四海

Chen-kao-chün 鎮嵩軍

Ch'en-liu hsien 陳留縣

chen-ming t'ien-tzu 真命天子

Ch'en Te-hsing 陳德馨

Ch'en Tu-hsiu 陳獨秀

cheng 正

Ch'eng-an hsien 成安縣

Cheng-chou 鄭州

Cheng-hsien 正縣

Ch'eng-tu hsien 成都縣

Cheng-yang hsien 正陽縣

Chi En-ming 齊恩銘

Chi-hsien 汲縣

ch'i-hsing pi-lu-fu 七星避塵符

Chi Hung-ch'ang 吉鴻昌

Chi-nan 濟南

Chi-ning hsien 濟寧縣

Chi-tung hsien 濟東縣

Chi-tze hsien 雞澤縣

chia 甲

Chia-hsiang hsien 嘉祥縣

chiang-shen fu-t'i 降神附體

Chiao-tung 膠東

chieh-pai hsiung-ti 結拜兄弟

ch'ien-ch'eng tzu-ling 前成司令

Ch'ien-ch'i-ssu 潛溪寺

Chih-hsien 莘縣

Chih-hsien 支縣

Chihli 直隸

chih-tui-chang 支隊長

Chin 金

Chin Feng-yao 金逢耀

Chin-k'ang chiang 金剛將

chin-luan-tien 金鑾殿

Chin-t'ung yü-nü 金童玉女

Chin wu-shen 金五神

Chin Yün-p'eng 靳雲鶚

Ch'ing-hsien 景縣

Ch'ing-hsien 青縣

Ch'ing-lung 青龍

Ch'ing-p'ing hsien 清平縣

Ch'ing-tao-hui 青刀會

Chou Fu-sheng 周佛生

Chou Kung-tzu 周公子

Chou Ting 周定

Chou Tsung-ch'ang 周宗昌

ch'ü 區

Ch'ü-chang 區長

Chu Chin-k'ang 朱金剛

Chu Hsiang 朱香

ch'ü-hsien 衢縣

Chu Hung-teng 朱紅燈

chu-jen wei-yüan 主人委員

Chu-ke Liang 諸葛亮

Chu-ma-tien 駐馬店

ch'u-pao an-liang t'i-t'ien
hsing-tao 除暴安良
替天行道

chuan-shih 全史

chuang-shen-tzu 裝身子

Ch'üeh-shan hsien 確山縣

chün 君

Chün (city) 郡

chung hung-hsüeh 中紅學

chung-yang-tao 中央道

Chung-yang tzu-chih-chün
中央自治軍

erh-yeh 二爺

fa-ch'i 法氣

fa-shih 法師

fa-t'ang 法堂

fa-t'i 法體

fa-t'ung 法童

fan-t'i 凡體

fang 方

Fang Ch'ang 方昌

fang-tsung 方總

Fei-hsien 肥縣

Feng Te-hsing 馮德馨

Feng-tien 奉天

Feng-yang hsien 鳳陽縣

Feng Yü-hsiang 馮玉祥

Fu-an 福安

fu-fa wu-pien 佛法無邊

Fu Sheng-hsün 傅繩勳

Fu-shun 撫順

fu-t'ang 佛堂

Han Chih-nan 韓指南

Han Fu-sheng 韓復生

Han Yü-k'un 憨玉琨

Han Yü-ming 韓欲明

hao-i 好義

Hei-ch'iang-hui 黑槍會

Hei-hu 黑虎

hei-hu-ch'ang 黑虎長

Hei-hu-tao 黑虎道

Hei-lung-chiang 黑龍江

Hei-lung kuan 黑龍關

hei-teng-chao 黑燈罩

Ho Ch'ien-chin 郝千金

Ho-fei 合肥

Ho Meng-keng 何夢庚

Honan 河南

Ho-nan wu-chuang nung-min tai-piao ta-hui 河南武莊農民代表大會

Hopei 河北

Ho Wen-liang 賀文良

Hou Tzu-ching 猴子精

Hsi-hsia hsien 棲霞縣

Hsi-hsien 息縣

Hsi-kuang ts'un 西廣材

Hsi-p'ing hsien 西平縣

Hsi-yu chi 西遊記

Hsia-chin hsien 夏津縣

hsiang 鄉

hsiao-hung hsüeh 小紅學

Hsiao-tao-hui 小刀會

hsiao-tui-chang 小隊長

Hsieh Wen-tung 謝溫東

Hsieh Yü-t'ien 謝玉田

hsien-tan 仙丹

hsin 心

Hsin-an hsien 信安縣

Hsin-ho hsien 新河縣

Hsin-tsan hsien 新蔡縣

Hsin-yang hsien 信陽縣

Hsin-yeh hsien 新野縣

hsiu-ts'ai 秀才

Hsiu-wu hsien 修武縣

Hsü-ch'ang 許昌

Hsü Yao-ts'ai 徐耀才

Hsüan-wu ta-ti 宣武大帝

hsüeh 學

hsüeh-chang 學場

hsüeh-t'ang 學堂

Hu Ching-i 胡景翼

Hu Ch'üan-lu 胡全祿

Hu Jih-ch'ing 胡日清

Hu Kuei 胡貴

Hu Te-chün 胡德俊

Hu Tse-li 胡澤禮

Hua-lan-hui 花籃會

Huang-ch'iang hui 黃槍會

Huang-ch'uan 黃川

Huang-chou 黃州

Huang-hsüeh-hui 黃學會

huang-hua 黃華

Huang Ling-chi 黃陵集

huang-men 黃門

Huang-sha 黃沙

Huang-sha-hui 黃沙會

Huang Sheng-ts'ai 黃生才

Huang Wen-ch'ing 黃文清

hui 會

hui-chang 會長

Hui-min hsien 惠民縣

hui-t'ang 會堂

hui-yu 會友

Hunan 湖南

Hung-ch'iang-hui 紅槍會

hung-hsüeh 紅學

Hung-hsüeh-hui 紅學會

Hung-men-hui 洪門會

hung-teng-chao 紅燈罩

Huo-shan 霍山

i-chün 毅軍

I-ho t'uan 義和團

I-ho-t'uan yen-chiu 義和團研究

I Sheng-lei 一聲雷

I-yang 宜陽

I-yung-chün 義勇軍

Jen-i-hui 仁義會

Ju-hsien 汝縣

k'ai-fang-ch'ang 開防場

K'ai-feng 開封

k'ai-yen 開眼

Kansu 甘肅

Kao Chün 高峻

Kao Hsien-chou 高憲周

kao-liang 高梁

Kao-t'ang hsien 高塘縣

Ke-lao-hui 哥老會

Kiangsu 江蘇

Kirin 吉林

K'ou Ying-chieh 寇英傑

Ku-ch'eng hsien 故城縣

kua-yen 掛眼

k'uai-pao-ch'ang 快跑場

k'uai-tao 快道

Kuan-hsien 冠縣

Kuan-kung 關公

Kuan-sheng ti-chün 關聖帝君

Kuan-t'ao hsien 館陶縣

kuan-yin 觀音

Kuan-yin lao-mu 觀音老母

Kuan Yün-ch'ang 關雲長

Kuang-p'ing hsien 廣平縣

Kuang-shui 廣水

Kuangtung 廣東

Kuei-she-chiang 龜蛇將

Kueichou 貴州

kuei-she-chiang 龜蛇將

Kung Ching-han 龔景瀚

kung-fu 工夫

kung-fu che 工夫者

Kung-hsien 宮縣

Kung-hsien 鞏縣

Kuo Chin-pang 郭金榜

Kuo Hsien-chou 郭憲周

Kuo Hung-pin 郭鴻濱

kuo-min 國民

Kuo-san ts'un 郭三村

Lan-tzu hui 籃子會

lao-shih 老師

Lao-fu ch'ang 老佛廠

Lao t'ien-yeh 老天爺

Lao-yang jen 老洋人

Li Chia-yen 老甲寅

Li Ch'ing-lung 李啟龍

Li En-kuan 厲恩官

Li Hsiang-fen

Li Hui 李憓

Li Hung-chang 李鴻章

Li Hung-ch'ou 李鴻疇

Li Jun-p'u 李潤普

Li Jung-heng 李榮亨

Li Kuang-yen 李光炎

Li Kung-ts'ai 李公寀

Li P'ei-ying 李培英

Li San-ma-tzu 李三麻子

Li-shan lao-mu 黎山老母

Li Ta-chao 李大釗

Li ta-fa-shih 黎大法師

li-t'ang 禮堂

Li Tao-ho 李道和

Li T'ien-ch'ih 李天池

Li Wan-ju 李萬如

Li Yüan-ching 李元慶

lien-chang 連長

Lien-chuang-hui 聯莊會

Lien-ts'un-hui 聯村會

Lin-chang hsien 臨漳縣

Lin-ch'ing 臨清

Lin-chü hsien 臨朐縣

Lin-hsien 林縣

Lin-ying hsien 臨潁縣

Ling-hsien 陵縣

Ling-ju hsien 臨汝縣

Ling-kuan 靈官

Liu-an 六安

Liu Chen-hua 劉鎮華

Liu Ch'i-hei 劉七黑

Liu Ch'i-yen 劉啟彥

Liu Ching-k'ai 劉慶凱

Liu Hsi-hsien 劉希賢

Liu Hu-tzu 劉鬍子

Liu Kuei-t'ang 劉桂棠

Liu San 劉三

Liu Shih-tuan 劉士端

Liu-ting liu-chia 六丁六甲

Liu Wen-yen 劉文彥

Liu Yün-ho 劉韻珂

Lo Mei-chi 羅敏齊

Lo-ning 洛寧

Lo-shan hsien 羅山縣

Lo-yang 洛陽

Lo-yüan 羅源

Lou Pai-hsün 婁白循

lu 路

lü-chang 旅長

Lü-ch'iang hui 綠槍會

Lu-chou hsien 廬州縣

Lu Heng-an Lü-i-hui 呂恒安綠纓會

Lu Kuei 路貴

Lu-shih hsien 廬氏縣

Lu Yen-sha 盧延沙

Lu-yung-hui 綠纓會

lung-men-t'ou 龍門頭

Ma Chan-shan 馬占山

Ma Fei-t'ien 馬飛天

Ma Hsiang-te 馬尚德

Ma-tzu 馬祖

mai-cheng ping 賣征兵

Manchukuo 滿洲國

man-ming ting-t'i 冒名頂替

Mao Hung-pin 毛鴻賓

Mei-hua ch'üan-hui 梅花拳會

Meng-yin hsien 夢陰縣

Miao Chin-sheng 苗金聲

Miao-tao hui[a] 妙道會

Miao-tao hui[b] 廟道會

Min-sheng ch'iu-chi tzu-chih

hui chün 民生救濟自治會軍

mou 敵

Nan-chün 南軍

Nan-ho hsien 南和縣

Nan Hua-wen 南化文

Nan-kung hsien 南宮縣

Nan-yang hsien 南陽縣

nei-ch'ang 內廠

Nien 捻

Ning-te 寧德

Ogata Tomasaburō 緒方知三郎

Ou-yang Ping-yen 歐陽炳炎

p'ai 牌

p'ai 排

Pai-ch'iang-hui 白槍會

Pai-li hsien 勃利縣

pai-lien-chiao 白蓮教

Pai-shih-kang 白石岡

Pai-ying-hui 白纓會

pan 班

P'ang San-chieh 龐三傑

pao 保

pao-chia 保甲

Pao-ch'ing hsien 寶清縣

pao-wei-t'uan 保衛團

Pei-fang hsüan-t'ien ta-ti chen-wu 北方玄天大帝真巫

Pen-hsi 本溪

P'eng Kuei-lin 彭桂林

P'eng Yi-chu 彭以竺

Pien-liang 汴梁

p'ing-ch'ang 平場

P'ing-yüan 平原

Po-p'ing hsien 博平縣

san-ch'ang 三場

San-kuo yen-i 三國演義

sha 殺

Sha-ho hsien 沙河縣

Shan-hai 山海

Shansi 山西

Shantung 山東

Shan-tzu-hui 扇子會

shang-fa 上法

shang-hsüeh 上學

shang-i 尚義

she 社

she-chiang 蛇將

shen-ping 神兵

shen-shu 神術

Shensi 陝西

shen-t'ai 神台

sheng-ti lao-yeh 聖帝老爺

shih 師

shih-erl lo-han 十二羅漢

Shih Hua-nan 實化南

shih-ti 師弟

shih-yeh 師爺

Shih Yu-san 石友三

shou-ch'iang 授槍

Shou-chou hsien 壽州縣

shou-wang-she 守望社

Shuang-tao-hui 雙刀會

Shui-hu-chuan 水滸傳

Su-ch'ien hsien 宿遷縣

Su-hsien 蘇縣

Sui-p'ing hsien 遂平縣

Sun Chih 孫直

Sun Hsiang-ch'i 孫祥麒

Sun Hun-you 孫渾有

Sung 宗

Sung Chiang 宗江

sung-fa 送法

Sung-pang 松潘

sung-shen 送神

Sung-tzu Kuan-yin 送子觀音

Szecnuan 四川

szu-ling 司令

szu-ling-pu 司令部

Szu-p'ing hsien 四平縣

Ta-ch'ing 大清

ta fa-shih 大法師

Ta-ming hsien 大名縣

ta-shih-hsiung 大師兄

Ta-tao-hui 大刀會

ta-tui-chang 大隊長

ta-yeh 大爺

T'ai-chi-hui 太極會

T'ai-ho hsien 太和縣

T'ai-k'ang hsien 太康縣

T'ai-p'ing 太平

T'ai-shang lao-chün
太上老君

Tan-tao-hui 單刀會

T'ang-yin-hsün kung-lu
湯陰佾公路

T'ao-hua hsien 桃花縣

Tao-kuang 道光

tao-t'ai 道台

tao-yu 道友

Te-hsien 德縣

Te Leng-t'ai 德楞泰

Teng-feng 登封

Teng Liang-sheng 鄧良生

Teng Yen-ta 鄧演達

t'iao 挑

t'ieh-kuan-chao 鐵關罩

t'ien-men-chiao 添門教

T'ien-men-hui 天門會

T'ien-ping 天兵

T'ien-ti-hui 天地會

T'ien Tsai-t'ien 田在田

t'ien-tzu 天祖

t'ien-wang 天王

T'ien-yeh-tao 天爺道

t'ing 亭

ting-chia k'ai-shan
丁甲開山

Ting Hsiang-ling 丁香玲

Ting Shou-ts'un 丁守存

tou 都

t'ou 頭

Ts'ai Yung-fa 蔡永發

ts'an-mo-chang 參謀長

Ts'ao-hsien 曹縣

Tseng Kua 曾振

Tseng Li-ch'ang 曾立昌

tsung cheng-chih pu
總政治部

tsung-chiao-shih 總教師

Tsung-chih-hui 總指揮

tsung-fang-chang 總方戈

Tsung-hui 總會

tsung-hui-chang 總會長

tsung-szu-ling 總司令

tsung-t'ou 總頭

tsung-t'uan-shih 總團師

Tu 杜

Tu Chiao 杜喬羽

tu-pan 督辦

tu-pan kung-shu 督辦公署

tuan 段

t'uan 團

t'uan-chang 團長

t'uan-tsung 團總

tui 隊

tui-chang 隊長

t'ui-fa 退法

tui-lien 對聯

t'ung 統

Tung-ch'i hsien 東杞縣

T'ung-hua hsien 通化縣

Tung-ming hsien 東明縣

Tung-nan hsien 東南縣

Tung-p'ing hsien 東平縣

Tung Szu-hai 董四海

Tung Tzu-hsiang 董子祥

Tung-wu-pao 東五保

T'zu-chou 磁州

T'zu-hsien Tzu-shih lao-yeh 磁縣祖師老爺

Tzu-t'ung hsien 梓桐縣

Wan Fu-lin 萬福臨

Wang Ch'eng-chang 王成章

Wang Chih-ch'i 王治岐

Wang Chih-kang 王之剛

Wang Ching-jen 王慶仁

Wang Fu-ch'ing 王輔清

Wang Hsiao-ch'ü 王少渠

Wang Hsing-pang 王興邦

Wang-kuei hsien 望奎縣

Wang K'un-ju 王坤如

Wang Kung-t'ang 王拱棠

Wang Lao-wu 王老五

Wang Lien-san 王連三

Wang Shou-hsin 王守信

Wang-t'ai 王台

Wang-tou hsien 望都縣

Wang Tung-ch'eng 王東城

Wang Tze-hsien 王澤顯

Wang Tzu-ch'eng 王自成

Wang Yüan-shan 王元善

Wei I-san 魏益三

Wen-ch'ang ti-chün 文昌帝君

wen-hsiang 聞香

wen-shih 文師

wen-t'uan-pu 文團部

wu 伍

Wu-chih-hui 無極會

Wu Chün-sheng 吳俊陞

Wu-hsia 巫峽

Wu-kan-shen 五杆神

Wu-kuang ta-ti 武光大帝

We lei-k'ang 五雷剛

Wu-liang-fu 無量佛

Wu P'ei-fu 吳佩孚

Wu-t'ai shan 五台山

Wu-ting 武定

wu-t'uan-pu 武團部

Wu-yang hsien 舞陽縣

Ya-lu (river) 鴨綠江

yamen 衙門

Yang Chen-yü 楊振宇

Yang Kuan-i 楊貫一

Yang Kuo-hsin 楊國新

Yang-wu hsien 陽武縣

Yao Pin-shuang 姚賓雙

Yeh-hsien 葉縣

Yen-ch'eng 郾城

Yen-chin hsien 延津縣

Yen-lin hsien 鄢陵縣

Yen-shih 偃師

Yen Yü-hui 延玉會

yin[a] 陰

Yin[b] 殷

Yin Tzu-hsin 尹子鑫

ying-chang 營長

Ying-shan 英山

ying-tu-tui 硬肚隊

yü 鬱

Yü (river) 御河

Yü Ch'ang-hai 于長海

Yü Feng-k'uei 于鳳魁斗

Yü-huang lao-yeh 玉皇老爺

Yü-huang ta-ti 玉皇大帝

Yu-ts'un 油村

Yüan Shih-k'ai 袁世凱

Yüeh En-p'u 岳恩溥

Yüeh-ling 樂陵

Yüeh Wei-chün 岳維峻

Yün-liang fu-ho 運量佛哈

Yung-nien hsien 永年縣

Yunnan 雲南

Michigan Monographs in Chinese Studies

51. *Career Patterns in the Ch'ing Dynasty: The Office of Governor-general,* by Raymond Chu and William G. Saywell.

Michigan Abstracts of Chinese and Japanese Works on Chinese History

1. *The Ming Tribute Grain System,* by Hoshi Ayao, translated by Mark Elvin.

2. *Commerce and Society in Sung China,* by Shiba Yoshinobu, translated by Mark Elvin.

3. *Transport in Transition: The Evolution of Traditional Shipping in China,* translated by Andrew Watson.

4. *Japanese Perspectives on China's Early Modernization: A Bibliographical Survey,* by K. H. Kim.

5. *The Silk Industry in Ch'ing China,* by Shih Min-hsiung, translated by E-tu Zen Sun.

6. *The Pawnshop in China,* by T. S. Whelan.

The Michigan Monographs and Michigan Abstracts series are available from:

Center for Chinese Studies Publications
The University of Michigan
104 Lane Hall

Printed and bound by CPI Group (UK) Ltd, Croydon, CR0 4YY

13/04/2025

14656529-0005